The Color of Dusk

The Color of Dusk

An Autobiography

Phyllis Demarecaux

THE COLOR OF DUSK
AN AUTOBIOGRAPHY

Copyright © 2016 Phyllis Demarecaux.

All rights reserved. No part of this book may be used or reproduced by any means, graphic, electronic, or mechanical, including photocopying, recording, taping or by any information storage retrieval system without the written permission of the author except in the case of brief quotations embodied in critical articles and reviews.

iUniverse books may be ordered through booksellers or by contacting:

iUniverse
1663 Liberty Drive
Bloomington, IN 47403
www.iuniverse.com
1-800-Authors (1-800-288-4677)

Because of the dynamic nature of the Internet, any web addresses or links contained in this book may have changed since publication and may no longer be valid. The views expressed in this work are solely those of the author and do not necessarily reflect the views of the publisher, and the publisher hereby disclaims any responsibility for them.

Any people depicted in stock imagery provided by Thinkstock are models, and such images are being used for illustrative purposes only. Certain stock imagery © Thinkstock.

Author's note
Extracts from The Maid's Room are included with permission of myself, the author

ISBN: 978-1-4917-9623-8 (sc)
ISBN: 978-1-4917-9624-5 (hc)
ISBN: 978-1-4917-9625-2 (e)

Library of Congress Control Number: 2016907986

Print information available on the last page.

iUniverse rev. date: 10/06/2016

CHAPTER ONE

Life can be a lonely journey when you start outliving all those closest to you which is why it's a good idea, beginning at twenty, to make at least one new friend a year. I like to think I made it clear to those who are gone, just how much they meant to me and how great their contribution was to my survival before they bit the dust, but it's hard to tell. We weren't raised in a demonstrative family.

My journey began the 12th of December 1931. The sister who preceded me was three years my senior. It is probably because of her presence that I have a few rare memories of the farm we lived on. The first one must date somewhere around my second birthday. The oldest son of a friend of our parents was visiting. Sister Jane was seated on his lap and I decided I wanted to be there. It was a struggle as I recall, because Jane was where she wanted to be and did not relish sharing. Our parents laughed about my infatuation and undoubtedly made some comments about the possibilities of my future behavior. (For reference and in case he's still around, the young man's name was Shumway. He was a teenager at the time.)

The second memory is more visual than emotional. Our mother was standing on a wooden flatbed with two iron rimmed wooden barrels being pulled by a team of horses which meant she was on her way to get water. I remember running across a grassy knoll toward her, calling out in whatever blather children do when they don't talk but loud enough to be heard. She pulled in the reins and the team came to a halt. She picked me up and sat me on top of one of the

Phyllis Demarecaux

barrels in front of her. "Want to come with me, do you," she said with an understanding grin. I remember smiling my satisfaction and we were off to another forgotten adventure.

In my third memory, Jane and I were wrestling on the sofa when suddenly I felt an urge to go to the bathroom and announced my need. "Pee pee," I said. "Pee pee." She stopped the wrestling and said, "Pee in my hair." So I did, at which point she called out to our mother with great indignation. Why was she so upset? I merely did what she told me to do.

Big sisters can be devious. I know because when our younger brother and sister were born, I also became a "big sister".

We left the farm when I was about three. I remember our father explaining to Jane and myself that he had to sell our Shetland ponies. We were moving into a town where there wouldn't be any place for them to stay. A pony needs green grass and lots of fresh air, he said. In retrospect, I think selling the horses was much harder on him than on us.

Jane had started school while we were still on the farm. A siege of outbreaks, bothersome, boil-like growths on the top of her head caused her to miss several weeks of school. The doctor finally suggested to our mother that she bathe the boils with peroxide. The result was blonde hair in spots but the boils were disappearing. Eventually Mom just poured peroxide all over her head. Jane became the only peroxide blonde in the first grade.

She was still a blonde when we moved to Sidney, Montana. I remember her first day in the new school. We were living in a basement apartment on the north end of Main Street. I went looking for her. Not having found her, I thought I was on my way home when I came across a stairwell leading downward. It was, in fact, an outside stairwell to the basement of one of the town's principal clothing stores, the Yellowstone Mercantile. Our mother caught up with me before I got to the bottom of the stairs and went to a great deal of trouble explaining to me why I couldn't go to school with Jane.

2

The Color of Dusk

We lived in Sidney long enough for our brother Darrel and sister Sharon to be born then we moved back onto the reservation in Wolf Point where our father joined a partnership business with a man named Jim Sullivan.

Jane, still blonde, was transferred into a new school for the third time. She eventually managed to finish up the first grade but, in her words, she liked it so much she did it again. Her failure was blamed on all the moving around we'd done plus the amount of time she'd missed classes because of boils which were healed long before her hair returned to it s natural color.

Our mother was an East Band, blue-eyed, Cherokee from Pryor Creek, Indian Territory, Oklahoma. Her mother, my grandmother, was born Bessie Bickford, one of ten children. Her parents were John Henry Bickford and Nancy Dephyona (or Delfina) Gulley. Nancy's father, Bessie's grandfather, a Pentecosal preacher, was Cherokee.

Grandpa, Alburton Brown, was about 6'3", a svelte figure and something of a ladies man. He was fifty or fifty-five years old when, on November 7th, 1905, he married our twenty year old grandmother.

Prior to Grandma Bessie, he'd been married to Cole Younger's sister. Assuming our research is correct, he married our grandmother within days after Cole's sister's death. Two sons from that marriage lived with Bessie and him for an indeterminate period of time.

Alburton Brown was also Indian. We have no record of Grandpa's tribal origin and correspondence with the Department of Interior, Commission to the Five Civilized Tribes concerning a couple parcels of land in Pryor Creek, Indian Territory, do not specify. He was disputing ownership of a claim located in Pryor Creek and was advised to take his claim to the Cherokee Land Office. It is therefore likely that he, too, was Cherokee.

Whatever he was, he had imagination, ambition, a gutsy disposition and a pass-for-white complexion which eventually made him eligible for a Montana Homestead.

The family left Pryor Creek with two sons, Tilly and Duke, and a three year old daughter (our mother) for Montana where they settled on a Homestead in the Lambert area. Our mother's sister, Florence and brother, Jesse, were added to the brood and the entire family remained there until our mother married Emory F. McMorris and moved to Wolf Point. Tilly and Duke also married but lived pretty much in the proximity of the homestead until our grandfather's death in 1940.

Grandpa, a major fan of Jessie James, delighted us with bloodcurdling stories about his rides with Jessie. Research from another family member indicates he rode with Quintel's raiders. It is believed that fear of being discovered is why he delayed applying for the land grant in Montana. There is, however, no real confirmation. He would have us believe that he rode with Jessie in his younger days. It is quite likely that he met Jessie through his marriage to Cole Younger's sister. The James brothers formed their group around 1866 at which time our grandfather would have been approximately sixteen years old. They started young in those days, so there is also a strong possibility his stories of the gang were true. Our *Nez Perce'* Indian Aunt, Margaret Brown, who rode her tractor-mower every summer up to her 97th year of life, said there was no question about his riding with James. She told one of grandpa's favorite stories about Banker's foreclosures and Jessie's intervention.

As was his custom, Jessie supplied the necessary cash. "Make an appointment for the payoff," he'd say, "And let me know when he's coming." When the Banker, smiling his satisfaction, started home, his pockets lined with the cash payoff, Jessie was waiting. "What goes around comes around." Unfortunately our mother walked in on one of Grandpa's stories and put a stop to it. She did not want him frightening us with the stories of the past.

We hadn't been frightened. We'd been fascinated but Grandpa never talked to us much after mom's tirade.

Like many Cherokees, Grandma was light skinned, light enough to "pass for white" which, in those days, is what she chose to do. It was a white man's world. Indians like ourselves were, and sometimes

The Color of Dusk

still are, referred to as half-breeds. Many white men still think it's their world but they're living in the past. Today's world population is definitely colored.

Jane and myself share our father's color. Not quite as white as he, but definitely pass-for-white and lighter than our younger sister and brothers. At our father's suggestion, Mom, who had no birth certificate, registered us as white on our birth certificates.

Dad was Irish, born in Illinois. He and an older brother, Elvie, had the "Go west, young man" itch and both wound up in Montana. Evie's family spent a few years in Wolf Point, then moved to Harden, Montana where they settled and remained for life.

Home in Wolf Point turned out to be in the redesigned loft of a huge classically red livery barn located just one block off Main Street. Our father's business was set up on the ground floor. We were four siblings now. There were three comfortable years between Jane and myself, but Darrel, Sharon and I were a baby-a-year close. Mother had her hands full.

We loved the new home. After the tranquility and semi-cloistered solitude of farm life, this new home was an endlessly exciting festival of activity. There were more cars on the street at any given moment than we had seen in our combined lifetimes. Mom enjoyed sharing the excitement of street life with us and put Sharon's crib near the loft window so that we might all be together. Darrel, too young to appreciate the radical aspect of the change in our environment, was less drawn to the window. He mostly entertained himself. When he did venture into 'our' area it was generally to steal baby Sharon's bottle. He'd bite holes in the nipple so when we gave the bottle back to the baby, it would end up soaking her in milk.

Jane and I used the loft window to survey the comings and goings of the corner grocer. We'd wait until he was in the back of the store to rush down and steal cookies from the outside bins lining the storefront. He was aware of our game, of course, and when, inevitably, we became too greedy, threatened us with jail. That ended our life as thieves.

Phyllis Demarecaux

When the circus came to town one of the "Barkers" set up a hamburger stand on the corner of main street approximately ten yards from our barn. Jane remembers his bark even today. "Hamburgers! Red Hot! Onions in the middle and pickles on top!" We waltzed around his stand a good deal, and it paid off in the end. When the circus closed down, he gave us the remainder of his hamburger. We were ecstatic. Our parents prepared a picnic for us and all was going well until Jane bit into her burger and uncovered a very resentful, vindictive, worm who stuck his head out to see what was going on.

Jane, of course, was back to school again. Kids in school weren't so kind to the new girl in class. They called her - and the rest of us - barnyard chickens but the tomboy side of Jane soon set them straight. She was anything but "chicken".

Our Aunt Florence, mom's younger sister, came to visit us while we were living in the barn. Just six years older than Jane, she was fun to have around. A tornado hit while she was there. We all took refuge in an abandoned jail house located about half a block from the livery barn. It was a small one room jail. The concrete walls were at least a foot thick. A single barred, narrow, horizontal shaped, window just below ceiling level, allowed the only light. There were no furnishings. No bed. No cot. No chair. Our father picked Jane up so that she could see out the window. Florence was kind enough to lift me up to the window so that I, too, could see what the tornado was doing to our home. The barn was shaking, but it wasn't going anywhere. I have no idea how long we were there nor do I remember any damage to the barn.

Jane remembers hearing our father say the barn had been lifted and set down approximately six inches off its original foundation. Others, in the outlying areas, were not so lucky.

I also remember the day we had a chimney fire. Mom was cooking our noon hour meal when the area at the ceiling around the stove pipe caught fire. She began battling the flames with a large towel but to little avail because she wasn't tall enough to reach the source. We all watched in fascination as the flames began to spread.

6

The Color of Dusk

Mom began shouting our father's name. Lucky for us he was in his downstairs office and responded to the urgency of her call. Within minutes of his arrival, the flames were doused with a pail of water. Lunch was soupy, but we were all happy campers. Our father had saved the day.

It wasn't so long after the fire that we barnyard chickens moved into a real house, still on the South side of town. (Many towns in the West were divided by the railroad tracks. In this case the South side of town was the white man's and a few affluent Indians's world. *South,* even in today's world seems to imply 'better'. (My current home town has a 'South Hill' that fits the description.)

It was in this house that I almost choked to death on the skinny little bone in the chicken drumstick. While Jane and our cousin, Delly were laughing themselves sick, my parents realized I was in serious trouble. There was no hemlock knowledge in those days so they grabbed me and went to the outside porch where my mother held me upside down by my ankles while my father beat on my back. It took two or three good whops on the back before the bone in my throat dislodged. I came to, coughing, sputtering and swinging back and forth. My mother was calling out, "Not so hard, Emory. I'll drop her."

The good next door neighbor called the police and reported that my parents were beating me, but we got it straightened out. Until I became a vegetarian, a chicken breast was the closest I got to a chicken leg.

The cousin, Delly, Aunt Margaret's son, was with us because he had rheumatic fever and was being treated by a local doctor. His parents lived on a farm some thirty or forty miles away and could not afford, either financially or time-wise, to make the trip daily. While Delly was there, our mother came down with diptheria and the bunch of us was quarantined. Our father used to sneak in through the window after dark and left for work well before sunup. With so many mouths to feed, there was no way he could give up work for such a long time.

Phyllis Demarecaux

One of the local churches was good to us during the quarantine. When Christmas rolled around, they rang our doorbell and ran, having left a large bag of toys for us. It was one of the richest Christmas' we had in those early years.

The neighbors on the other side of our house were something else.

We didn't really get to know their son until well after the quarantine and summer rolled around.

Junior, he was called. "Ornery as the day is long," I recall my mother saying. He and Jane had climbed up on the roof of the garage attached to Junior's home and, at his father's request, were throwing down pieces of lumber. They were doing a good job and were almost finished when Junior spotted me and told me that I would get hit if I didn't move. I shook my head "No". I was safe, I reasoned. The other pieces hadn't hit me. "This one is going to hit you," Jr. announced as he raised his arm and threw the well-aimed piece of two-by-four.

The geyser of blood was blinding me and I was furious. I stomped my way into the house, using my fists to keep the blood from my eyes. Our mother was in the living room hosting a sewing bee. One of the women actually screamed when she saw me.

I don't remember the trip to the doctor. (No emergency centers in those days.) He said the semi-soft spot on my head had burst open.

I do remember his stitching up my head. The area had probably been numbed or perhaps it was numbed from the blunt force which broke it open in the first place. I could see the thread, or whatever it was that he was using to stitch my skin back together. I don't recall having any pain to complain about, maybe because I was so interested in what he was doing. A needle and thread to sew up my head!

The "accident" did get me some recognition in the neighborhood as everyone seemed to know what had happened. Did Junior go into low profile? I don't remember. Did his parent apologize for their son's behavior? I don't think so.

The Color of Dusk

Some weeks later on a warm summer evening, the window in the kitchen eating area was open; the dinner table had been set. A large rock flew through the open window, hit the tablecloth and dragged everything that was on it onto the floor with a great clatter. Broken glass flew everywhere. (Plastic kitchenware was not yet on the market, not in our small town.) Jane spotted Junior running for his house, picked up the rock from the floor, which now had his name on it and with lightning speed, rushed out the back door in an effort to intercept him. He was in the house by the time she got there, but Jane has always been a patient person. She waited quietly, calmly and when Junior thrust his head out the window to do the usual open mouth, tongued "N'ya, n'ya, n'ya" she socked him a good one. Not having removed the rock in her fist, Junior's screams of excruciating pain were the result of a shattered nose. His rock throwing "N'ya, n'ya, n'ya" days were over.

It wasn't long after the rock incident that we moved to a new home near the railroad tracks. It sat next door to the main North Side convenience store. Our neighbors were French. At least the lady of the house was French. I remember her charming accent and her patience with us. She allowed us to dunk our bread into the hot chocolate, something our mother told us we were not to do in polite company. The French know how to enjoy a *tartine*. (I still dunk them in my *cafe' au lait* when taking it *sur le zinc* in Paris.) I also remember that Mom greatly admired the incredibly styled *chignon* our French lady was able to manufacture with layers of her long, long hair.

It was while living in this house that I remember getting my first doll for Christmas. She had a sawdust filled body with a crier which said, "Mama" when I bent her over. Little sister, Sharon, had one, too. It was her doll that we operated on in order to find out what made the doll cry. Of course Sharon cried because we couldn't get her doll sewn back together. Our mother fixed it, but we'd thoroughly destroyed the crier. If I remember correctly my punishment was to exchange my doll for hers, but, of course, once it had stopped crying, I lost interest.

Phyllis Demarecaux

It was also a year when I received a double layer of chocolate covered cherries for my birthday. I hugged the box to me, making sure no one was going to invade it's contents. Punishment for my unwillingness to share came by way of a major upset stomach. I gladly gave up the second layer and cannot, to this day, stomach the chocolate covered cherry.

Life was moving on. We left the rented house and moved to the north hill into a foreclosure house that was purchased by our parents. Our father was quite gleeful at having acquired the house under the very nose of the banker who had set up the foreclosure. He, the banker, had at least a half dozen properties, purchased through bankruptcies. He didn't need another. It was a small one bedroom home sitting on an exceptionally large landscaped double lot. There was a well defined entrance, a large double living room, half of which served as the children's bedroom, a single bedroom for our parents, an ample eat-in kitchen and a closed-in back porch which ran the entire width of the structure. There was also a telephone, still connected, in the living room. The day we moved in Mom was sitting on a chair next to it. I was sitting on the floor at her feet listening, fascinated, as she read a list of groceries for delivery to the house. It was magic. She explained to us that we wouldn't be keeping the phone, but that right now it was helping her because she had so much work to do in the house there wasn't time to go shopping, even for food. Our father soon reported to the telephone company and the service was disconnected. In just days, Jane and I were stringing copper wire, supplied by our father, to empty produce cans, happy with our very own telephone system.

The purchase of the foreclosure was a financial stretch and left the family with meals of dehydrated vegetable crumbs which our mother threw into boiling water to create a soup. It wasn't long before the mere smell of it gave me the dry heaves. Our parents' solution was bread and milk. We each had a small glass of milk and one slice of bread. (Such was life in the great Depression.)

The Color of Dusk

Jane recalls asking why we couldn't have something else to eat. Seeing the hurt expression on our father's face, she never asked again.

It was about three and a half months before my 6th birthday that I started school. The schoolhouse was a sad looking structure with a black tarpapered roof. We walked through a set of large double doors and made our way down an exceptionally wide stairwell to the basement. It was not an above-the-ground basement. There were windows high up along one wall of the room. We could look outside and see the weather, but not much of anything else. The teacher, Bertha Hass, told us we would not have the luxury of blaming outdoor distractions on our failure to respond to her questions. She was tall, but she couldn't see much more through those windows than we could.

The only thing I remember about the layout of the classroom was a piano no one ever played in the far corner of the room. Ms. Hass made us stand behind it when we talked too much in class. I never had to stay very long because I learned how to make the keys ping. The pinging was apparently more distracting than my silly whispers.

The city was building a new school for grades one through four on a large lot just behind our new home. There was going to be a playground so large that we could use it for a kid-sized baseball diamond. Construction was completed and the school opened by the time I was in the second grade. Everything here was above ground.

There was considerable talk in town about keeping the basement school for the Indians and using the new school for white students. Common sense won. Keeping both schools open would have meant extra expenditure at a time when people were still pulling themselves up by the bootstraps of the great depression. I don't know what would have happened in our case if the city had voted for segregation, but they didn't, so we were all together in the new school.

On one of those warm summer afternoons, I was playing alone in my parent's bedroom, where I had no business being, that I ran into trouble.

Phyllis Demarecaux

For whatever reason I was attempting to unplug a lamp. I grabbed the cord and gave it an impatient tug. The wires in the plug came loose, but not enough to break the connection. I was caught up in the current, unable to let go, issuing wildly unintelligible "uh, uh, uhs" in rhythm with the alternating current. It was strong enough to hold me but not enough to throw me loose.

Our mother, having heard my cries, rushed in, stopped short when she saw me and took immediate stock of what was happening. To me it was slow motion but in reality a mere second or two. She raised her leg, planted her rubber soled shoe on my chest and, in a single thrust, sent my body flying across the room. It was a lesson well learned. Never again did I enter my parent's bedroom to do my mischief. And I ALWAYS, when disconnecting any electrical apparatus, pull on the plug and not the cord.

Our father's business was prospering. I was in the second grade when he made it his business to locate the prior owner of the foreclosed home he had purchased for $50.00. She was in California and gratefully received the $500.00 he sent, thus putting father's conscious at rest.

Prosperity also meant he could work on an idea he had. He built a vine covered arbor on the back lot of our house, plowed up the earth inside the arbor and planted ginseng. The ginseng thrived. People came from out of town and out of state to inspect the crop. Most were astonished to see it doing so well. They had thought the Montana growing season would not allow enough time to keep the plants alive.

Hot summer days our mother used to take a chair into the coolness of the arbor and do her mending. She darned our socks, replaced missing buttons, sewed up torn sleeves and faulty hems. The place was her little secret, a place where peace and quiet were welcome companions. She usually left the arbor about the time we were due to come home from school. (4 pm)

Another luxury we had was the newly built WPA toilet on the edge of the property. The problem with its location was that every

The Color of Dusk

other kid on recess in the school yard was able to climb the fence and use our facilities. It actually got to the point where we kept the toilet paper in the house.

Aunt Florence moved in with us for a time. She was going to high school, a luxury our mother never had. Mom had gotten through the eighth grade before grandfather pulled her back home to help on the farm.

Our father never made it past the third grade. He was, however, a mathematical genius with a calculator in his head but useless for helping me with those tricky written math questions. I'd read them to him and he'd give me the answer. "How did you come to that conclusion?" I'd ask.

"Used my head," would be his reply. He could measure a tank's length and circumference and know how many gallons it would hold without ever putting pen to paper. A zero to him was an "ought". I can hear his voice even today as he made his calculations. … "with an ought, ought, and ought after the dot and…."

The neighboring Forestness family was great. They had three boys. Gilman, Maurice and 'Two-ton' Tony. Gilman was three or four years older than I.. Maurice was in my class at school and 'Two-ton' was pre-school. I had a major crush on Gilman. He went to the South side school, so had to have been at least a fifth grader. Whatever the difference in our ages, he was kind of smitten with me and some of the kids razed him about it. He was the first person to ask me for a 'date'. He asked me to go to the movies. Tuesday night was "Pal Night". Admission was two for a nickel. The movie started at four. Our mother was amused but hesitant. I was too young, she said, but she would allow me to go to the movie if Jane could come with us. I don't know how it worked out money wise, but Maurice, Jane, Gilman and I went to the movie.

There was another young man to whom I took a shine. He was a classmate from the first through the fourth grade. His name was Douglas Ren. (I don't actually remember his color but his name tells me he was probably an Indian.) Douglas lived further away, so we

Phyllis Demarecaux

didn't see each other often, but he did come visiting from time to time. Gilman didn't like Douglas so I tried to have him over when Gilman wasn't around. In the end, Gilman's family moved away.

The local movie theater was doing drawings once a week. The winning name won a hundred dollars. Movies were a rare occasion and I don't recall under what circumstances Jane and I happened to be there when my name was drawn. Mom bought new dresses for us girls. The remainder, I'm sure, went to put food on the table and to pay the grocer who allowed us to run a charge account when times were tough.

After the fourth grade I was bused along with my sister to a school on the South Side of town. Douglas didn't transfer with me. Perhaps his parents pulled him out of school, perhaps they moved. I never saw him again.

The South Side was different. Classes were larger; students less friendly. Of course, the bulk of them had been together for years and the majority were white. It was we North Side students who were the intruders.

Wednesday afternoons were for Christian study. Students were given the choice of going to church or staying in school. Mom's brother Tilly and his wife had visited recently, excited about a new religion they had been introduced to. There wasn't any church for the Seventh Day Adventists so they met in each others homes every Saturday. We'd gone to visit them and although our mother was interested, our father didn't seem to be. I thought our uncle Tilly's excitement was worth looking into so when the school asked for my choice, I chose church - or I should say - churches. Every week I'd go with another classmate, to another church.

There were almost two dozen denominations in our small town. Each one had its own rules but the goal they preached was pretty much the same. They all talked about God and/or Jesus and the Bible, but they hadn't gotten their act together when it came to interpretation, which is probably the reason I was able to figure out, while still quite young, that most of the rules were man made. The

The Color of Dusk

most important lesson I seemed to have come away with was that God's son, Jesus, was the person to talk to if you needed something and if you behaved yourself and remained faithful, there was a pretty good chance of getting it.

In one of the churches a lady who was telling us Bible stories requested those of us who were saved to raise our hands. I gave this some serious thought and decided not to raise my hand. Everyone else seemed to know as their excited hands were waving in the air. The young lady singled me out, of course. Didn't I know if I'd been saved? No, I told her. "I don't know. Sometimes I do things I shouldn't, even if I try to be good." She gave me a tender smile and suggested I raise my hand because, she said, she was sure that I was also saved.

Another thing the churches seemed to have in common, aside from knowing who was or who wasn't saved, was the little bedtime "Now I lay me down to sleep" prayer that our mother had taught us.

On one occasion Jane and I, quite unintentionally, gave our parents a serious fright. The thermometer was reading 40 degrees below zero and we were "missing". Having surmised that the school bus was once again not going to show up, we had decided to walk home. We were feeling good about having learned and correctly recited the 23rd Psalm but not so good about the Preacher. Our hearts were with his son. His father had made him stand before our class and read the 23rd Psalm. The boy had a major stuttering problem and the stress his father was putting him under only made it worse. The father's pained expression as he prompted his son along added to the unintentional cruelty. Young as we were, we prayed for both of them.

It began snowing early on. Great white flakes fell from the sky adding to the accumulation of previous days. They glittered in the street lights as the skies darkened. We were catching them on our gloves and studying the infinite detail of their different shapes. Unaware of our parent's dilemma, we took our merry old time. We flopped onto the snow piles and made angels, threw snow balls at each other and waltzed about in the lamp light. When our parents

Phyllis Demarecaux

finally found us, we were just a few blocks from home. They'd gone by us two or three times, they said, without seeing us. Perhaps it was those times we lay in the snow admiring the unending supply of flakes being offered from the sky.

Because the school bus regularly failed to pick us up, something which, in those cold winter days, our parents did not appreciate, we ended up going to the Pentecostal Church next door to our father's new business. We lived on the North Side so the bus driver's "oversight" was understandable. Most North Side students were either "poor" or Indian. We were a bit of both. (At the time we didn't even think of race as being the reason, so my making that remark must come from something I later learned from the world of grownups. They should not be proud of it.)

The next door pastor was on good terms with our father. He dropped in regularly to share a shot of whiskey at the end of a working day. While not yet a heavy drinker, our father was not above an occasional wingding. He was also not above stepping out on our mother. At one time he even brought the woman's two sons to our place for Mom to baby sit.

One of the sons was a hemophiliac and required special attention.

It was their family's return to Wolf Point that provoked a memory of earlier years. I recall that their mother was wearing riding breeches and swinging a riding crop with a grand flair. I did not find her attractive. Our mother couldn't have been completely unaware of something going on because I heard her say in a low tone as though talking to herself, "And she's never been on a horse."

The memorable occasion her visit provoked was one in which our father took me with him on his tryst. I was young and was not yet talking. They were in the back seat of the car. I was in front eating selected chocolate candies from the stock my father had stuffed into the glove compartment. Anything to keep me quiet. I didn't understand what was going on but I wasn't comfortable with whatever it was. I particularly didn't like her remark: "Did you have to bring that brat with you?"

The Color of Dusk

Note here that while I understood her words and their meaning, I didn't begin talking in a serious way until I was about four years old. My first words had been spoken during one of my mom's sewing bees. All the ladies laughed and cooed over it and begged me to say it again. "It was sooooo cute." They made such a fuss that I was determined I would not speak again until I could put together a proper sentence which, once again, proves that when a child begins talking, he/she has been understanding what is being said for at least a year. Why do parents not understand the logic of something so simple? I'm certain my father would have been horror stricken had he realized I understood their conversation, what little there was of it. Lucky for him understanding is not necessarily knowing and knowing is not necessarily understanding.

Summers Jane and I became master mud pie makers. Mom would supply us with Calcimine for the toppings. (Calcimine was a white powder which, mixed with water, became the popular and least expensive way to do indoor painting.) For our purposes the Calcimine made great frosting for our mud cakes, ice cream sodas etc. We also raised winter onions and sold them. Our usual charge, at Mom's suggestion, was a safety pin or two.

Jane and I wrote a couple "musicals" to which we invited the neighbors and their children. I remember one old sheer curtain which Mom gave to me for a dance number, which, of course, was a big hit.

From where the ideas for all this came, I cannot remember. We did have a small radio in the house but other than a pal-night serial on something or other like Zoro in black and white, we had never been to a full length movie. The first time I can remember talk about a full length movie was in 1939. I was seven years old. The oldest daughter of the neighboring family was ecstatic about "Gone With the Wind" and it was actually in color!

Jane was outgrowing me, and somewhere in there, my attention turned to younger sister, Sharon. Unlike Jane, Sharon enjoyed playing with paper dolls. We invented any number of stories for them and were constantly changing their clothes, a great introduction to the ready-to-wear business. No wonder we grow up thinking we need large wardrobes and oversized, walk-in closets.

The neighbors across the street also had two younger daughters, Helen and Nettie. Jane spent a good deal of time playing with Helen. The two of them enjoyed spying on Nettie and myself. I recall Nettie attempting to teach me to play dominoes. She kept winning. I couldn't understand her rules. They kept changing. It was at this moment Helen, with Jane, thrust her head around the corner of the house and declared, "You'll never learn the game if Nettie doesn't stop cheating."

She was right. I never learned to play dominoes.

One other experience I recall when going to the grocery store with a girlfriend who was going to buy a candy bar and had promised to share with me. The candy selection was in the front window of the store. I watched and waited while she hovered over the area, watching as she hummed, touching, first one than another candy bar. "I am having, trouble deciding," she told us.

"Chocolate is probably the best," I offered helpfully.

"Yes," she agreed. "I think so, too." She selected a chocolate bar, smiled at the grocer and followed him back to the cash register where he rang up her purchase.

I was excited about getting some chocolate, a rare treat for any of us. Once outside and several feet beyond the grocery store, she reached down the front of her dress and pulled out of a handful of candy. I was flabbergasted. I'd been standing right beside her and hadn't noticed a thing. The grocer hadn't either, but he must certainly have suspected something. I remember, in retrospect, that she had tightened the belt on her dress before we walked into the store. Now I knew why. I also understood why she bent over so far while making her selection. Our mother's response, when I told her about the light fingered thievery, was to encourage me to look for a new friend.

The Color of Dusk

My new friend's name was Carolyn Stinger. The Stinger family lived just a few houses down from us. Our mom was really happy about it when they moved in. She had been a childhood friend of Carolyn's mother whose name was also Grace. The two Graces had spent a great deal of time on horseback in their early years. It was through Mrs. Stinger that we learned of our mother's prowess on horseback. Our father told us that he wouldn't go into the stable with some of the horses that our mother used to ride. I remember begging mother to take a ride when some friend brought a horse to our house. She did and we were awestruck.

Carolyn had two older sisters, Ella and Doris. Ella and Jane were also friendly and Doris, sandwiched in between, spent time with both of us. Their little brother, Dale, was younger than myself by perhaps two years. I remember a time at our house when a group of us were testing fright levels by jumping off the back of a pickup (parked in our driveway) from a standing position. This may not sound frightening to you, but it did to me at the time. I managed to do it, but it seemed very high standing up on the back of that pickup. Today, at my age, I climb down using the bumper. It wouldn't occur to me to try to jump.

Dale was watching us and like all younger kids, wanted to do what the 'big' kids were doing. Someone lifted him up onto the pickup bed, I don't remember who. I went to take hold of his hand.

Having experienced my own fear, I felt Dale was too young to be subjected to our foolishness. Dale, however, rejected the helping hand. He would do it alone. Already macho at his age.

He jumped.

His knees buckled when he hit the ground and he rolled into the bumper of a car that was parked behind the pickup. I went to him and helped him up. He brushed himself off and said he was okay but he wasn't.

I never saw Dale again.

Our parents, protecting us from the realities of life, weren't talking to us about adult things, so it was a few days before I learned

Phyllis Demarecaux

Dale had died. Because the doctor was unable to diagnose what the problem had been, our father suggested they request an autopsy.

Their findings said that Dale's rib cage had caved in and was pressing against his lungs. Because of this his body was not getting a sufficient amount of oxygen into the blood stream. Dale died because he was oxygen deprived.

I remember my father talking to our mother about what the doctor had told them: had they known the source of the problem, pressure on the rib cage would quite possibly have forced Dale to gasp for air and it was likely that his gasp would have been strong enough to push those soft baby boned ribs back where they belonged.

Dale's fall, his hitting the bumper on that parked car, was not probably, but almost certainly the source of the problem. I don't know if I would have realized what Dale's problem was, had I known he was "sick". I do know it is a memory that will always be with me.

CHAPTER TWO

December 7th, 1941, Pearl Harbor, war and the voice of President Franklin Delano Roosevelt on the radio was dominating the air and our lives. Our father recalled his friend, Wayne Lamberton, predicting that Japan, our biggest scrap iron buyer at the time, would soon be sending it back to us. Wayne, a pilot, carried the U.S. air mail from place to place. Younger than our father, Wayne enlisted but died in a plane crash before he was able to serve. Our father rushed to enlist in spite of our mother's pleading that he not do it. He was turned down. Four children and 41 years of age made him too much of a risk and too old. He would have to do what he could for the war effort on this continent. We were a long way from the war, a long way from industrial cities.

The only time I ever remember Dad staying home alone to watch us was when Mom had volunteered to help roll bandages for the Red Cross. She was wearing a soft print dress, a black topcoat and a jaunty black pillbox. She was also wearing lipstick. I was definitely intimidated by this new look and remember telling her very shyly that she looked very, very nice. Everyone agreed and she smiled with pleasure.

Dad's contribution to the war effort was mountains of scrap metal. Early 1942 our father sold his share of the business in Wolf Point to his partner, sold our home on the North Side and moved the family to Sidney, Montana where he had taken over the franchise of the Pacific Hide and Fur. For us children the move meant the

Phyllis Demarecaux

loss of an Indian culture, more inter-woven into our lives than we either knew or understood. The warm comfort of belonging invoked by the Indian nature was not the style of these new people. Our introduction to this new life was to become a true confrontation with 'real life'.

It was somewhere around this time that our Grandfather ended up in the hospital. I was with Mom when she went to see him. He was lamenting his loss of weight, his inability to stand up by himself. He complained that his strength had completely deteriorated. He must have died soon after my visit. I don't recall having attended his funeral although I do know that he was buried in the graveyard at Lambert, Montana. Dad had an obsidian glass sculpture made with Grandpa's name in it and left it as a grave marker. (They've become quite valuable collector's items and the marker was stolen sometime in the seventies). Our Grandmother left the Homestead after Grandpa died. She moved into Sidney where she shared a home with Jesse, her youngest bachelor son. Tilly, Duke and Jesse were not farmers and neither was our father so the Homestead was taken over by our Aunt Florence and her husband, George Reimann. Aunt Florence's choice was to pay off big time in the seventies when the oil companies came.

Jane and I were in the yard of our new home in Sidney one bright early fall morning when a truck with a half dozen school kids in back, pulled up. The driver stuck his head out the window and called to us. Did we want to help top sugar beets? Of course we did and rushed in to get Mom's permission. Although she was okay with Jane, she was hesitant about me, I was only ten, but she finally agreed and we were on our way. Schools were closed during beet harvest. With all our young men gone to war, students were needed to help get the crops out of the ground.

The beets were plowed up and stacked in rows with a long wide flat path between them. The knives they gave us were about a foot long with an extremely sharp two inch wide blade and a curved hook on the end. We used the hook to pick up the beet, then grabbed it

22

The Color of Dusk

with our other hand, whacked the greens off the top and threw it into the path.

It was hard work. A good sugar beet with the top on it can easily weigh 30 pounds, sometimes 40, and a person can work up a good appetite. The farmer's wife provided an abundant and delicious lunch for which we were charged by the amount we ate, the total cost being held back from our pay check. For Jane our first beet topping venture became an unforgettable memory. Her pay check, after meals, came to $2.50. As to the amount of my own check, I simply do not remember. Jane thinks it may have been as much as forty dollars.

Our schools now, were separate. Sharon and Darrel in the third and fourth grades, were in an elementary school. I was in a middle school, sixth grade, and Jane, in the Junior and Senior high school, was in the eighth grade. Once again there was some confusion about Jane. Unknown to her, they'd placed her in a seventh grade class. She was a whiz at math, especially the fractions, and was leaving her new classmates in a state of grudging admiration as well as a high level of resentment. Their mistake was discovered before the end of the day. The seventh grade teacher announced the error to a roomful of grateful students, thus restoring their dignity, and Jane was forgiven for being a genius.

When the first report cards came around, Jane's reported her usual Wolf Point grade: F (meaning failure) She was accustomed to getting Fs for the same work, copied by her classmates who got As in Wolf Point. A classmate with whom she was visiting was astonished when Jane showed her the F, and said it had to be an error. She insisted it was a mistake and took Jane's report card to the teacher for verification. It was an error. The teacher was extremely apologetic. Jane's grade was an A.

My own experience in the new class that first day was a spelling test. I had four errors. In Wolf Point four errors for me meant an F so when the teacher looked through the student's papers and spoke

Phyllis Demarecaux

my name aloud, I made myself as small as possible. It turned out he was making an example of me for having done so well!

Goodness me. Maybe things would be different in Sidney!

Years later, teacher Ethyl Page, told us that she had refused to work in places where teachers were given the names of students of prominent families who were to be treated "with care". We, Jane and I, decided Wolf Point must have been one of those towns, which is not to say that Sidney was above lowering its own standard of high mindedness on occasion.

The house we were living in that first year heralded a pot bellied stove in the living room. It's also unlikely that the building had ever been insulated. We moved out of there as soon as the weather permitted. This time into Craigo's Cabins, small, but well insulated and well heated. It was to be a temporary home, but it lasted a full winter. It was the year our mother became pregnant with brother Michael.

By now we had a pet, a beautiful angora cat which we named Angela. Business was going well for our father. He brought home the cash each night and allowed us, Jane, Sharon, Darrel and I, to count the coins for him. We were proud of the confidence he placed in us.

It was while we were living in the Cabins that our father brought home a curly haired black man. A boy actually, about 18 or 19 years old. He was working his way to the west coast and had stopped in at the Hide and Fur for a temporary job. My father hired him and brought him home to eat with us because the local restaurants wouldn't allow him in. I'm not talking about the South here, I'm talking about Montana which sits on the southern border of Canada. The year was 1943.

He was a great tease, the young man. I remember he told me some wild story about salt and pepper and he let me run my hands through his silky curls. His skin color was lighter than many of the Indians on the reservation where we had lived, but I did realize there was a difference between his color and that of the Indians. He explained to me that he was a negro and laughed when I asked

24

The Color of Dusk

him if he lived on a reservation like we did. We thoroughly enjoyed his company. He wasn't around very long. Our town was not a comfortable place for him to be, which left me with a sadness that I was still too young to completely understand.

June of 1943 brought in a major unexpected snow storm. Angela was lost. She'd been outside when the storm hit. We were confined to the cabin for three days before we could get out to search for her but she was never found.

The wind had piled drifts of snow as much as twelve to fifteen feet high. We enjoyed walking around on top the roof of the cabins behind ours. It was in the cabin at the end of the lot that we heard a man's voice calling for help. The snow was packed so high that the door of his cabin was not even visible. We rushed back to the house to tell our mother and soon there was a rescue team on the way. He was an older man who had been unable to get out for three days and was without anything to eat.

Late Spring rolled around and put us on the move again. Not far. Just across the highway. It was a large two story stone house known locally as the Vaux house.

Sharon and Darrel each had their own smaller bedroom and Jane and I shared a larger room on the upper floor. Closets in the bedrooms were so large that at one point, Sharon put her single bed into the closet so she could have more room to play.

A single oversized bathroom was also on the upper level. Our parent's bedroom on the ground floor was to the right of the entrance hall. To the left was a more than ample sized living room. The formal dining room, behind the living room, had a long pass-through to the kitchen which could be left open or closed, depending upon the preference. The kitchen was also generously endowed with a walk-in pantry almost as spacious as the upstairs bathroom.

August and Darrel was wanting his duffle bag hung. We chose a large lower branch on a tree in the front yard. As many times as we threw up the rope we were unable to get it over the branch. My solution was to get a chair from the kitchen. It was a straight backed chair with knobs on each side of the risers. We plunked the chair down and I climbed aboard.

Darrel handed me the rope. I stretched up and with a little jump, threw it over the branch. The shift of my weight on the chair, which was not sitting level (one leg on the ground, three on the concrete sidewalk) caused it to tip. I lost my balance and fell onto the knob. My legs weren't long enough to touch the ground. The pain was excruciating. I fainted.

The next thing I became aware of was the doctor talking to my mother. The bone was very bruised and I would probably have a great deal of pain when trying to evacuate my bowels, but I would be okay. Fortunately, I could have hit the knob in such a way as to have it enter either the anal or the vaginal passage which, according to the doctor, would have caused much greater and possibly permanent, damage. The doctor's main concern, however, was our pregnant mother. It was she who lifted me up off the chair and carried me in. Michael Darwin, our baby brother, was due any day. He was actually born a week later.

Sister Sharon was not a happy camper. She had been the baby of the family for over eight years. Probably feeling unwanted and superfluous with the new baby getting all the attention, she decided to run away. She was about two miles from home, on her way toward Fairview, when she stopped at the Bach's home to ask for a drink of water. Mr. Bach humored her, then convinced her that with darkness falling she would be better off with a ride. Of course, he brought her home. She was apparently satisfied with whatever Mom told her because she never ran away again.

Mick, as we called our little Irish Indian brother, was four or five months old when we moved into a duplex house on Lincoln Street. Three upstairs bedrooms were put at our disposition. This time Sharon and I shared a room. Jane and Darrel were in smaller, separate bedrooms. Our parents used the enclosed front porch as their and baby Mick's bedroom and the outside door to the kitchen became the principle entrance. The third bedroom would later be temporarily rented to one of our teachers, Cyril Little, who was seeking a more permanent home for himself and his family.

Downstairs consisted of a middle sized eat-in kitchen, a double living/dining room area, a bathroom and the porch. Upstairs, there was a small storage area on each side of the stairwell. In time it was discovered by Sharon and her new friend, Ellie, who lived on the other side of the duplex. Together they pulled out the partition so that the two areas joined and it was in there that they spent hours playing paper dolls. Ellie, who was called at that time, "Toutee", had informed her parents that she would no longer respond to such a stupid name and was giving her mother a hard time because she no longer came when called. Eventually her mother gave in and Toutee became Ellie.

I was in the seventh grade now with a Montana History teacher, Jo Rogers, who had taught Jane as well as our mother when she was in school. Miss Rogers was an interesting, fabulous teacher. The fact that she had lived through much of the kind of life experiences she was teaching brought it all to life. She told us about the days when the steam boats ran up the Missouri. Classes would be dismissed so that students could help round up much needed wood to help keep the boats on the move. They were exciting days. It was not only the students who came to meet the boats, it was entire villages, towns, settlements. (Sidney is in Eastern Montana and sits at the junction of the Yellowstone/Missouri river valley.)

Rosemary Leveno was the heroine of our English class that year. Our teacher heard her use the word mischievous and corrected her pronunciation. "It should be mischievous, with a long e sound", she said.

Rosemary told her timidly but assertively, that she was wrong. "It should be pronounced with a short i sound. The e remains silent," she said. The teacher told her to go home, look it up in the dictionary and come back to class the next day prepared to make an apology.

The class next day had barely settled down when the teacher called upon Rosemary for her apology. "I am sorry," Rosemary

Phyllis Demarecaux

began. We all held our breaths. Would she word her apology in a manner that would please our teacher? "but," Rosemary continued. "You are mistaken. My pronunciation is the correct one." The room silence was absolute, not a whisper, sigh or cough. Our stunned teacher, after a second or two of paralysis, reached for the dictionary on her desk. "I will show you," she said. The only sound now in the room was the rustle of the pages as she turned them in search of 'mischievous'. She studied the page quietly, closed the book and carefully placed it back on her desk. "It seems," she said, "that I owe you an apology, Rosemary. Will you please accept it?"

CHAPTER THREE

We'd barely settled into the duplex when a circus/carnival came to town. Jane had gone to the grocery store with our Aunt Florence. Sharon and I were sitting on the front stoop watching the practice in the football field across the street from the house. A car pulled up at the stop sign and, after a brief exchange in the car, the driver called to us. "Do you have a bedroom for rent? All the motels and hotels seem to be filled up."

Sharon and I exchanged glances, then replied. "Sure. We have room for you." Mom, who was now working full time for our father at the Hide and Fur office, was a bit taken aback when she came home, but she honored our decision. Turned out the men were "carnies" which might well have been why there were "no rooms available" in town. For some inexplicable reason "Carnies" were not considered good people.

One room was for one of the young men's parents. They had come down from Canada to visit their son. Two other rooms were occupied by the Carnival guys. The only one whose name we remember was a very tall, large fellow whom they all called Pee Wee. One of the fellows, it turned out, was from Williston, North Dakota. They were all incredibly appreciative and we had free rides on anything we wanted.

The extra bedroom actually came from the neighbors on the other side of the duplex. Their sons were all in the service and they had only two daughters at home, so the landlord told us that we were

Phyllis Demarecaux

welcome to make use of the extra bedroom anytime we needed. We needed.

Jane and I slept on the downstair sofa. No, it didn't make into a bed but we were slender, determined and young. It turned out fine.

Just after the carnival we had a surprise visit from two of the Stinger girls, friends from our Wolf Point days.. They were now living in Whitefish, Montana. I have no recollection of why they were in Sidney. Neither do I recall seeing either of their parents, so it's possible they just came for a visit to see us. Whatever it was, it introduced us to cigarettes. Ella smoked and she taught us how. Our parents both smoked. It was very "grown up", so we were, of course, intrigued and eventually, hooked.

We had a lot of fun doing nothing. I remember one day, sitting on the edge of the bed, I drew in a deep breath, then began panting as though frightened. Ella was immediately concerned. "What's the matter? She asked.

"If I hadn't taken that last breath, I would have died," I replied.

"You're right." The others all agreed. "You would have."

"Well don't do it while I'm here," was Ella's reply.

After the Stinger girls left Darrel's friend, Hank Butsloff, from Wolf Point, came to visit. Mom sent Sharon to spend time with Aunt Florence's girls during Hank's stay, because Darrel was concerned she would be following Hank and himself wherever they tried to go, whatever they tried to do.

Mom kept baby Mick with her at work. It was up to Jane and myself to get the dinner meal started. On this particular afternoon Jane was at the fairgrounds having a lesson in archery. I was having a good time helping Sharon's friend Ellie decorate a church basket for a money raising project. Darrel and Hank had been in the back yard. When they came in Darrel asked for permission to go to a friend's home to shoot some baskets. I told him it would be okay if he was sure to be back by six pm.

A very few minutes later I looked at the clock. I'd been having so much fun I'd failed to realize the time. I rushed to the door

30

The Color of Dusk

to call them back. They had already reached the far side of the football field. I could hear the faint tinkle of their laughter. I called but they didn't react. They were too far away to hear me. Well, I comforted myself, Darrel was always good about being home on time. I cleaned up the area around the window seat where Ellie and I had been working with the baskets and busied myself with pealing potatoes for dinner. Dad was a potato man. A meal wasn't a meal without them. He wouldn't be home this evening because he'd left for Glasgow that morning with a load of furs but the potato habit had become ingrained in us.

Mom showed up a little later than usual. She looked serious and hugged me to her. Then she told me that Darrel had drowned in the slush pond behind the sugar beet factory. The fire department had brought in a resuscitator but, she said, it was probably too late. He'd already been in the water too long. They were still looking for his body. Darrel's friends, Milton and Clarence Ellwein, Darrel Gobels, one of the Myers boys and Billy Norton had been with Hank and Darrel.

The Ellwein boys were the ones who had gone to the Hide and Fur to tell Mom what had happened. Darrel Gobels and Hank stayed at the slush pond to show the searchers roughly that part of the pond in which our brother had gone down. It would be another couple of hours before they found him. Our father still hadn't been located so Mom took me to the factory slush pond with her. She probably didn't want to be alone and there was no one else around to help.

Danny DeShaw had gone to the Fairgrounds to pick up Jane. He brought her to the pond to be with us. The divers recommended we all go home. Mom would be notified when necessary.

At home we found food had suddenly appeared on the table. Caring neighbors had been busy. We didn't lock our homes in those days. A lady named Evelyn Syring showed up. A friend of our father, she said. Mom seemed to know her. She expressed her sympathy

31

Phyllis Demarecaux

to all of us, one at a time, then left. The Sebring family, next door, brought over more food.

The diver, Hurly Carey eventually found Darrel's body in shallow water a mere five feet from shore. Apparently a hernia had ruptured. We later learned he'd grabbed for Hank which left Hank fighting for his own life. Somebody made a call to Hank's parents in Wolf Point and they were there to pick him up that same evening. He needed their reassuring presence. They later returned to Sidney for the funeral. Hank was suffering from nightmares, his mother said. He'd wake up at night screaming for Darrel. They felt the funeral would give him some closure. Counseling was not something people did in those days. I pray for Hank, even today, pray that he is not blaming himself for Darrel's death. It took me years to overcome my sense of guilt.

Our father had apparently not reached Glasgow. There was talk of a possible accident. By noon of the second day radio calls were being sent out every half hour. Jane and I sat in the car parked in front of the house and probably shocked the neighbors with our singing hymns and other songs. Any songs we could think of. Aunt Florence and Uncle Jesse brought Sharon back to Sidney. Mom took her to town and bought her a jacket to wear to the funeral. Later she took us to the funeral home to view the body. Darrel looked cold to me. He didn't look like Darrel. Mom said she was sorry they'd put him in a suit. "He never wore a suit," she said. "That's why he doesn't look like himself."

Our father showed up late afternoon of the third day.

The best defense being an offense, he attacked our mother. What kind of mother was she? Didn't she know how to take care of her children? How could she have let this happen?

It didn't take long to cool him down.

He hadn't heard the radio message until, on his way to Glasgow, the third day, he stopped in Culbertson, Mt. about 30 miles from home, for gas.

32

The Color of Dusk

Where had he been? Romping in some woman's bed in Fairview, just ten miles from home.

The funeral took place as Mom had scheduled it. Following the service, the procession left the church and wound its way through town toward the cemetery. Although school was still officially on summer holiday, we were overwhelmed to see hundreds of students lining the streets, block after block, paying homage to our brother. It was incredibly touching. Bertha Hass, our grade school teacher from Wolf Point as well as our father's former business partner and friend, Jim Sullivan, came to the funeral.

Divorce was not an option for our mother, an Indian with no birth certificate, therefore no social security number, no salary for the work she did at the Hide and Fur and four hungry children to feed. Who would hire her in this small town? Who could and still be legal?

One of the early complaints I recall having heard my father make to our mother was her lack of "sociability". She wouldn't drink with him and his friends. With Darrel gone, she pacified him and herself with alcohol. She became "social". It wasn't too long before those occasional weekend drinking bouts that my father so enjoyed, became inevitably, daily, and always with our now also alcoholic mother at his side.

The time following Darrel's death was not all a blur. Isolated incidents like the time some fellow in a truck on the highway beside our home was having trouble shifting gears. I watched with fascination, then went outside and called out to him, "You have to double clutch it, Sir." About the second time I shouted it, the sirens sounded. It was the police. This "gentleman" I was trying to help was, in fact, attempting to steal the truck and yes, in those days, trucks had to be double clutched.

There was also the year that Bob Hope opened his radio show with an off color joke about a baby girl who swallowed an open safety pin and didn't feel the prick until she was eighteen. We all laughed, but only our parents understood. Hope was cut off the air. I

33

Phyllis Demarecaux

don't recall for how long. In today's world it would be shrugged over. Our world in 1943 was a healthier, cleaner-minded place to live in.

It was the time of Gabriel Heater, the newscaster who, in spite of the war, opened his show with "There's good news tonight!" There was Jack Benny, Red Skelton and Tuesday nights with Amos and Andy and Fibber McGee and Molly. Sundays brought The Shadow. Who knows what evil lurks in the heart of men? The Shadow 'do', we'd all say enthusiastically. The big bands were coming in and I was learning to jitterbug. We rarely went to the movies. Radio, tap dancing and singing were our passion. We collected song magazines which were published monthly with the lyrics for all songs on the hit parade. Lyrics in those days were as important as who and how it was sung. There was a brief flirtation with motorcycle riding. That ended for me when some young man ran his bike up a pole on the high line and landed on the ground with the bike on top of him. Not worth it, I thought. It was also the year of the Normandy invasion.

I think having had a death in the family left us all better acquainted or if you will, more aware of our mortality than most teenagers and in the new life our mother was leading with our father, we were fast maturing. Fending for ourselves and cooking our own meals while our parents partied became a reality we accepted. We discovered we could count on each other more than we could count on our parents. When things really got bad a year or two later, we linked up with the mother of Jane Hass, a classmate of mine and a relative of our Wolf Point teacher. We seldom called on Mrs. Hass but it was great knowing we could, at any time and she would always be there.

The following summer a group of young soldiers found their way into our lives. They were stationed at a prison camp located on the highway between Sidney and Fairview, Montana. This particular day they were returning German soldiers to the camp in an open truck when a serious sized hail storm hit. They stopped the truck on the highway next to the house and our mother invited them in out of the storm. According to her about a quarter of the prisoners were

34

The Color of Dusk

still too young to shave. They were shy yet curious and murmured quietly to each other as they looked around, somewhat wide-eyed. Our home was a totally ordinary middle class home, but judging from their reaction, either very different from their own homes or surprisingly similar. Their guards, the Americans, averaging 19 to 23, were not much older.

A young man from Brooklyn named Bagdaddy, a Spaniard named Alvarez and Bill Hammer, a blonde from Roanoke, Virginia, on whom I had my first girlish crush, are the three I remember. The prison camp was located between Sidney and Fairview. A sterling bunch of young men who were gentlemen in every way. We swam with them at Vaux's dam, talked with them about their homes, their lives and, on at least one occasion, went to the movies. The movies I remember because I asked Hammer, as they all called him, to hold my hand. He was sweet to comply. His buddies razed him mercilessly. I was a mere 13 years old. He must have been around twenty. His behavior was impeccable. He knew how not to encourage a young girl's fantasies and to do it without breaking her heart.

The camp was there because they used the prisoners to help harvest the sugar beets. Once the crops were in, the prisoners were moved to destinations unknown. It had been a fun, memorable couple of months. Both Bagdaddy and Hammer came to the house to say goodbye.

We also had a lot of fun with our baby brother that summer. His tongue, when he cried, vibrated against the roof of his mouth like the string on a bass guitar. When I mentioned it to our mother, she rushed him to the doctor's office. It seemed he was tongue-tied. They had to clip his tongue so that it could reach his teeth. We had him walking at nine months. The three of us took him outside on the front lawn one Sunday and spent the afternoon making him walk from one to the other of us. By the time we finished he realized he could walk anywhere he wanted to go. Baby's understand so much more than we give them credit for.

35

CHAPTER FOUR

Family life was still changing. With Darrel gone things were never to be the same. Our mother continued working for our father at the Pacific Hide and Fur, but we could no longer count on her presence, or our father's presence at the dinner table.

This particular time, Mom told us that they, our father and herself, were going to be counting votes and would therefore, once again be too late for dinner. We should "make-do" and not wait up for them. Sharon, tired of their late night behavior, sneaked out of the house and went to the voting poles to check on them.

They weren't there. They never had been.

It was a shock to discover they lied to us. We knew our father was a Saturday night drinker, but we'd always been able to count on our mother. Now that she'd subscribed to her husband's desire for a more sociable wife, we were truly on our own.

Jane, sixteen, and myself, thirteen, probably handled the change in lifestyle better than Sharon, who was only ten. To some extent we understood our mother's dilemma, her impossible working situation. Sharon wouldn't understand until later. Our baby Michael, was to grow up never knowing what supposedly constituted a real family.

Jane and I began dating. My pleasure was dancing. I loved to dance and eventually found a partner in Don Baxter of Fairview, Montana who shared my enthusiasm. We preferred dancing to 'necking' and became a 'couple' because of our constancy. We had rhythm! I don't recall how long we'd been dating when I learned that

The Color of Dusk

Don had been seen dating another girl. Whatever reason he gave as an explanation for his behavior, for me our future as a couple was totally compromised.

He, Don, would not be aware of my feelings on the subject, nor would he understand the why of my reaction, but I knew. I related his action to that of my father's infidelity to our mother, both past and present. If he could not be faithful in dating, I theorized, he would certainly not be faithful in marriage.

After Don, there was a young man who worked in one of the local filling stations, also a Don. Don Downs. He was older than Don Baxter, perhaps by as much as three or four years. We danced. In fact, I remember a girl friend of mine told me that she had gotten up during the night, looked out the window and saw Don and I dancing under the street light at the corner of her home. I remember the evening very well.

We also exchanged ideas. On his days off he occasionally walked me home from school, carrying my trombone, but eventually, he wanted more than I was willing to give, so he, too, went out of my life. In fact, he went as far as California.

Our parents in those years, were totally lost to us. We were children they cared about but no longer cared for. Around my freshman year we moved into an executive railroad coach. Our father built an underground gas furnace for central heating and put an electric water pump into the kitchen but that's as modern as it got. The outhouse was back in style.

We immediately dubbed our new home "The Coach" and "The Coach" it forever remained. A gated wrought iron fence circled a small speaker's platform on either end of The Coach. One entered into the window-lined living room first. A single overhead bed fit into the wall above a built-in sofa on the far right of the room. A single bed/sofa was, along with a dresser and a small end table, the only additional furniture.

To the left, a window-lined hall lead past the master bedroom to the back where there was a dining area as well as a built-in booth/

Phyllis Demarecaux

table under another overhead bed which folded into the wall. On the right, beyond the dining area was the kitchen sink with a window above it, counter space, cupboards and an electric range.

The master bedroom separating the living area from the dining/kitchen area, was the only private bedroom. It was furnished with a double sized, built-in bed and once again, an overhead bed which folded into the wall. This room housed the Coach's only clothes closet.

When our parents went on one of their unannounced trips.… They'd taken our baby brother with them…Jane and I salvaged the non-functioning overhead light fixtures, beautiful brass lanterns, and sold them for grocery money. We later learned they had gone to the Black Hills.

I also recall a visit to a local bank manager. (It was Carl Bratton, owner, I think, of the Richland National Bank.) We needed money, I told him. Money for food and for the carnival. The Richland County Fair was on and Jane and I felt our younger sister, Sharon, should be able to go. I also suggested to him that if allowed to write checks, we could open the Hide and Fur to keep the business going. He thought that would be "okay" if we really felt we could handle it. As I recall he gave me a half dozen counter checks, had me write out one of them for twelve dollars and suggested I purchase the food first.

Sharon got to go to the Carnival and we got even luckier when Al Langdon, a drinking buddy of our parents showed up. Learning that we were on our own, Al declared himself reformed, sobered up and appointed himself our chief cook and bottle washer. He was an astonishing man, but mute when it came to his personal life. It was apparent that he had a superior education and someone, at sometime had told us that he was able to speak five languages, fluently. Jane and I opened the offices of Pacific Hide and Fur and kept up our energy with Al's cooking.

The only purchase I remember us making was a cow hide. We cut off the tail and the ears, weighed it, then docked the seller an additional ten percent for the waste. The seller, a local farmer, was

The Color of Dusk

getting such a kick out of our business acumen that he let us get away with it. I paid him with a check which, true to Bratton's word, was honored by the bank. As soon as he was out of the place we dragged the hide to the salt bin and threw it in. Jane jumped down into the bin, and spread the hide. Once that was done we were confronted with the gymnastics of getting her back up to floor level. We must have found a ladder. Together we sprinkled the hide with salt to prevent it from spoiling and called it a day.

Our father, when they returned, said maybe he should hire us to do the buying. We did a better job than he. He didn't turn it over to us, of course, but that winter we devoted many an evening or weekend packing frozen ground horse meat and meal. That venture didn't last long, the job too tough, the work area, unheated. Our mother actually stepped in and put her foot down.

A summer later Sharon and I decided to pay a visit to our father's former business partner in Wolf Point, some 80 miles west of Sidney. I was the driver. It was a '32 Ford pickup with a '33 motor. Dad had taught me how to drive on my 13th birthday because we lived a good distance from school. There was no busing for students who lived within the city limits. I had the use of the pickup. The state of Montana didn't require a driver's license in those days. I was fifteen when Montana passed a law requiring a drivers license. Sixteen was the minimum age set for having a license but I drove to the County Court house, parked the truck, went upstairs and lied about my age so we decided to go to Wolf Point.

The parents weren't around and I don't remember where Jane was when we made this decision. Our first initiative was to get the tank filled. Then we picked up a five gallon can and had it filled with extra gasoline as we had no idea how much it was going to take for our trip. We charged the fuel to our parent's account, signed the voucher and went on our way. The trip was uneventful and we arrived at Jim Sullivan's place of business before closing time. He was more than marginally astonished to see us. Too gentle a man to ask if we had come with our parent's blessing, he suggested it would be nice to call and let them know that we had arrived safely. He tried. Several times. But as usual, our parents were not spending a quiet evening at home.

He took us to the Shumway's home where we were dined and bedded in style. The very generous Shumway family consisted of approximately five or six boys and one girl, added to that number was the son and daughter of Jim Sullivan and Jim himself. The Shumway's generosity had invited Jim and his family into their home when Jim's wife died. It must have been an early death because I remember my father working with Jim when I was just starting school, at the age of five. Jim's family was, at that time, already living with the Shumways.

A hearty, joyful breakfast the next morning and we were on our way back to Sidney. There was one heart stopping moment on the drive back. The engine died. For whatever reason, I'll never know. We stopped. A couple of men working in a neighboring field waved at us. We smiled bravely, waved back and, with a prayer in my heart, I turned the key in the ignition. The engine fired up and we were on our way.

Somewhere in that year, the high school band had been scheduled to make a trip to Regina, Canada. I played trombone but had completely forgotten about the trip. It was only by chance that I was in the area when I noticed the bus parked in front of the school was loading. Our band director, Oran Strom, spotted me and motioned me over. "Are you going with us?" he asked. Unprepared as I was, no change of clothes, about thirty cents and a partial pack of cigarettes in my pocked, I stepped up into the bus.

I don't remember how long we were in Regina. It was probably a three day trip. At least two nights, for certain. I shared a room with a couple of girls. The first night, I was exhausted, dropped into bed and never woke up until the girls poked me in the ribs and asked me if I could snore a little less loudly. I remember mumbling something, "sure, just get me off my back." and rolling over to show them the result. I recall hearing laughter, but was too tired to participate.

The Color of Dusk

Someone must have loaned me money. One of the girls loaned me a change of clothes, and they all took me with them to a local dance, located if I recall correctly, in a youth hall. I also remember eating what was to me, a strange breakfast of sardines on toast. It left me unsatisfied and I recall thinking it was much too expensive. On the trip home I had the audacity to complain to Mr. Strom about his smoking in the bus. We were not allowed. Why would the rule not include him? My addiction, I told him was just as tormenting as his. The result of my inquiry was two smoking breaks on the way home. The bus stopped and we went outside, he self-consciously, to satisfy our cravings. My three day absence from home seemed to have gone unnoticed.

That summer, an acquaintance asked me for a date to go skating at the rink just outside Glendive. It would be a lot of fun, he told me, since he'd noticed that I often went to the local roller rink. I'd never dated him before but agreed because he was right. I loved to roller skate.

He must not have been a minor because we began the evening with a stop in one of the local bars. While he drank, I asked if he might give me a dime to play the slot machine. He did and I won a handful of change which I offered him. "No," he told me. "It's your money. You won it." I thanked him and stuck it in my pocket.

Once at the rink, he ran into a group of buddies and proceeded to push his way up to the bar with them. I went looking for a skating partner and discovered that sister Jane was also there. We visited. We skated. I went back to the bar to see if I was missed. Apparently not so I rejoined Jane's group. We skated some more. Time was marching on and eventually her friends decided to leave so I bid them good-bye and went in search of my date. He was nowhere to be found. I even had someone check the men's room. My date was not there. I rushed back to Jane's group but they were already gone. The crowd was rapidly diminishing and I realized if I didn't act fast, I'd be stuck, so I managed to hitch a ride, not to Sidney but into

Phyllis Demarecaux

Glendive. It was really an act of kindness because they would be going off toward Miles City, the opposite direction.

They dropped me off at the Greyhound Depot. I had to wait around, but thanks once again to God and my guardian angel, the slot machine winnings, were enough to pay for a ticket home.

The trip to Sidney wasn't exactly eventful, but it was memorable. Myself and the driver seemed to be the only people on the bus. Probably concerned at seeing someone my age traveling alone and in the wee hours of the morning, he asked me to sit up front, closer to him. I was without a coat and although it was summer, those early morning hours were cool. Aware of his concern I tried to answer his questions honestly without revealing too much about my home life. I told him my date had gotten drunk and forgotten me. It was just as well. He would have been too drunk to drive. Sunup was scrumptious. He told me about different sunrises and sunsets in other areas where he'd driven buses.

With nobody else on the bus, we first went to the post office where he dropped off packets of mail. From there he insisted on driving me to our front door. "I couldn't leave you alone at the bus stop at this time of the morning" he told me. "You'll be safer here." He nodded toward The Coach and remained watching me until I reached the door. I never forgot his kindness.

And did it ever give the busy/body who lived across from us something to talk about! We thought she never slept. She was always capable of telling our parents exactly what hours we girls were keeping. Whatever she told them, good or bad, it didn't seem to connect with our folks. And why would it? Our hours weren't any more erratic than theirs.

Betty Chadderdon tried to sponsor a membership in the Rainbow Club for my sister Jane. It didn't work, of course. The mighty few denied her membership offering her probable "inability to afford" the purchase of the formal required for the membership. They did not want to put her in and "embarrassing" situation. Reality? It wasn't the amount of money our parents had, it was the

42

The Color of Dusk

way they spent it that they were finding objectionable. Children almost always - especially in small towns - are more often than not - judged by their parents behavior. It's sort of like today's judicial system. You're pretty much guilty until proven innocent which is a lot harder to do, especially in today's world of television with popular shows which, in my opinion, are competing in the pre-trial conviction of the accused.

My senior year was capped with an appendectomy. They even removed a partial toothpick! My mother's timing and God's intervention, the day she came to visit me, undoubtedly saved my life. She walked in to discover that I was blue from lack of oxygen. Her shout for help came and within seconds a nurse was there with an oxygen tank. My teeth were clinched tightly shut and I was attempting to swallow my tongue, effectively suffocating myself. By now I was fighting their attempts to open my mouth. In an early state of euphoria, I was telling my guardian angel that I wanted to stay with her.

"You must go back." she told me.

"Will you let me come again?"

Apparently satisfied that she said yes, I stopped fighting the nurses' efforts. A clamp was placed on my tongue and an oxygen mask over my face.

I remember fighting them as clearly as yesterday because I DID NOT WANT to come back. You've all probably heard stories about people who claim to have seen a brilliant white light, an angel or Jesus who saved them. My bright light was surrounding an incredibly beautiful angel whose presence was more felt than seen. She was holding my hand, guiding me back to where I did not want to go. Our ability to communicate was most certainly an exchange of thought more than of words.

From that moment on, a day in my life has never passed without prayer.

My hospital room was not flooded with flowers and Russell Chadderdon, one of Betty's younger brothers, was the only classmate

Phyllis Demarecaux

who showed up to visit me. On a later occasion, Russell, surprisingly, also came to visit me when his father died. He picked me up in his car and we drove for two or three hours while he talked about his father. He had me in tears but was unable to produce any of his own.

The lack of attention from classmates wasn't surprising. We had many acquaintances but no real friends. Our parents were drunks which automatically made us the kind of girls 'nice' people did not want their children frequenting.

We were, as a result, each others best friends although until our move from Lincoln Street we had a fairly close relationship with our neighbor's daughter, Lola Mae Sebring. Lola Mae's father knew our parents before Darrel's death and was certainly aware of the changes that were taking place in our home. I'm sure he prayed for all of us every day.

Our first hand knowledge of what alcohol could do to a family, kept us clean. The single invitation the three of us had to a student hay ride was, Jane and I quickly realized, because they thought we'd show up with at least one bottle of booze. People like us, you know, would have easy access. They were wrong. Booze doesn't lie around unopened in a drunk's home which is why our parents did their drinking in bars. Some people air their problems publicly; others do it behind shaded windows and locked doors. 'Civilized' drinking is done at home where it's 'respectable'.

That we accepted the invitation is surprising when I look back on it. I imagine, however, that we were somewhat flattered. These kids were "good" kids from "good" families.

The adventure turned out to be a bunch of drunken teenagers playing the idea of "grown up". Then and now the average teenager's picture of adulthood is a glass of booze in one hand and a cigarette in the other and they can hardly wait to get there.

Our transportation was a truck, a red truck with a half load of hay. We parked somewhere in the middle of a field. Jane, Lola Mae and myself had gotten out of the truck and were enjoying each other's company. The rest of the group was busy passing a couple of

The Color of Dusk

bottles around, probably scotch. Fortunately we'd remained near the lowered tailgate because suddenly the motor roared into life. Jane and I managed to get into the truck. The two of us turned. Lola Mae was having trouble.

She had ahold on the tailgate but was losing her grip and with the tailgate down there was no leverage, no bumper, for her feet to find. In unspoken agreement, we each grabbed an arm and began pulling for all we were worth. By now the truck was accelerating into motion. It's bumpy ride wasn't helping. The rest of the group in the back of the truck were all standing, looking forward into the wind and shouting their exhilaration. There was no way we could get their attention.

My arm seemed to be pulling away from my shoulder blade but just as I felt my grip begin to slip I saw the unparalleled, genuinely terrified look on Lola Mae's face. Her expression added strength to my prayers and gave me a burst of power and with "One, Two, Three" shout, Jane and I pulled with all our combined might. The truck chose that moment to jump and bump and Lola Mae came sailing into our arms knocking us back into a hay-cushioned fall. Our driver had crossed the ditch and found the pavement. They were speeding their drunken way home.

Betty Chadderdon purchased a mimeograph machine and set up office behind Chadderdon's furniture store. She contacted Jane to handle the stencil cutting and a weekly newspaper was born. They called it the *Town Talk*. I whittled my way in by helping with the sale of advertising space. We did money raising drives for Red Cross, Cancer, etc., charging each advertiser one dollar for including his name on the list of donors. One page was usually sufficient. Ours was a small town, but being small also meant not wanting to be left out. The result was that almost every business contributed. As I recall, the total number of contributors was around eighty three. Sixty percent of the revenue went to the charity. Our father, having, by now, been relieved of his position at the Hide and Fur

Phyllis Demarecaux

(undoubtedly because of his drinking) had gone into the septic tank pumping business, Jane and I designed his ad with a banner announcement "Our Business is in the Hole". He loved it, adopted it and painted the slogan on the door of his truck.

The local barber loved it when we pinned his name across the top of his bald head in one of his ads.

By now, Betty had moved the business to roomier digs on lower Main Street.

My senior year I contributed my expertise to the *Town Talk* by writing the congratulatory message to the senior class with the usual upbeat, look to the future propaganda they fed us in those days and maybe still do, The *Town Talk* was distributed gratuitously to all homes and businesses by Boy Scout volunteers who earned badge points for helping. It became so popular that people actually called and complained when they didn't get their copy. Later on, Jane was to send shock waves through town by publishing the truth about a local automobile accident. Her headline:

LIQUOR INVOLVED IN ACCIDENT

That kind of reporting might be possible in a small town nowadays (They'd have to convince me.) but in the late 40's it was a giant 'No. No'

The first job I picked up following graduation was at the local JC Penny store. It was fun. I was given the responsibility of ordering ready-to-wear in the women's clothing department. Dresses, coats and hats. My voluntary sales pitch for the store was to purchase, at my employee discount, a hat for practically every day of the month. I loved hats and in one amazing month, we sold more dollars worth of hats than dresses!

Meanwhile, I continued dating Glenn Johnson, a young man who I'd met early in my senior year. Physically he was very much like Bill Hammer, the young soldier from Roanoke, the same approximate height, the same blonde hair, the same blue eyes. Glenn

46

The Color of Dusk

was a lineman working at the local REA, (Rural Electrification Association) He was visibly physically attracted to me. I was uncertain about wanting to spend my life with him but was at the same time attracted to him. He reminded me so much of my first love. Without any real experience, I came to believe that the painful erections he complained of were a sign of true love. He was laying a serious guilt trip on me. A conversation with my mother would probably have changed my life, but she wasn't around.

Glenn and I were married in August 1949 in a church in Glendive, Montana. I had insisted on a church wedding. The expression of disbelief on his face immediately following the ceremony did not bode well. "I'm sorry," I said.

Glenn chose his mother's home in Plentywood, Montana as a place to spend our wedding night. Although we had never discussed it, I thought he knew I was a virgin but apparently, he either didn't know, or didn't understand what that implied.

The next few months were a living hell but it wasn't until I missed my monthly that I went to see our local Doctor Beagle. I'll never forget the look on his face when he examined me. I was given a prescription which would help with the healing as well as the pain, and told to refrain from having sex for awhile.

While I spent my weekend re-washing his shirts for the fifth time which never quite made it to his satisfaction, he boozed it up with buddies. Once I read a letter one of his army buddies had written, his attitude toward me became understandable. The fellow was saying, "You were right. The girls out there (wherever he was) can be just as good as the ones we get at home. All you have to do is pull a gunnysack over their head."

Glenn left the REA and joined the union. From there he became a journeyman lineman, hired himself out to an outfit called something like Morrison Knudsen (The memory is faulty here.) They were electrifying rural Montana, Wyoming and Idaho. We began moving. And moving often. My loving husband was not

47

Phyllis Demarecaux

happy with my pregnancy. The day I made the mistake of sharing the baby's first moves, his reaction was a snarl, "You and that God-damned baby."

The doctor who had been treating me in the small town of Salmon, Idaho, seemed more interested in my lack of appetite than anything else. I don't remember him ever taking my blood pressure. I wasn't feeling particularly well but being pregnant, was only an "excuse" according to Glenn, who reminded me that he had been born in the "Wilds" of Canada and without a doctor being present.

It was the strange swelling in my legs that got my attention. I could punch my thigh and watch the indentation slowly disappear. I decided to show the neighbor lady, mother of three boys and get her advice. She counseled me to see another doctor. "Immediately," she said. "Today" and was on the telephone before I could explain to her that I had no money.

I was in a state of pre-eclampsia major toxemia, albumin, retention of fluid, accompanied by high blood pressure and, according to the new doctor, possibly leading to convulsions, coma and even death. He suggested I go to bed immediately and that I drink a least one 300cc glass of water every half hour, two if I could manage it. All salt was to be removed from my diet. "For life" he said.

Our son was born less than a week later on Saint Patrick's day, 1950. He was the first baby born in Salmon, Idaho's new hospital and normally I would have had a number of prizes which were being offered by the local merchants. However, it wasn't meant to be. Our son's fight for life lasted a mere thirty six hours. Somehow, somewhere, Glenn had picked up some feeling for the baby. Perhaps just seeing him. Anyway he asked the nursing staff to allow him to be the one to tell me that the baby had died.

It didn't work out that way.

I was in a room at the far end of a long hall. Voices seemed to come through a long hollow tunnel becoming louder as they overlapped.

The Color of Dusk

There was a hushed murmur. "She's sleeping now", then the whisper of clothing as the soft thump of measured footsteps approached my room. I remember rotating my head cautiously across the pillow and focusing my gaze expectantly on the open door. My visitor was a middle-aged woman in a crisp white uniform, with her triple black-banded cap perched at a jaunty angle. (Nurses in those days always wore a hat. The black bands indicated the level of their training.) She hesitated in the darkness of the doorway, I thrust my body to a seated position.

"My baby is dead."

She remained speechless.

"Isn't it?" I insisted. "My baby is dead."

"Yes," she said, inhaling deeply. "Your baby boy died during the night. No longer listening I slid beneath the protective gleaming whiteness of hospital sheets and turned my back to her. Later I felt the thrust of a needle. Then there was sleep.

Because I was an RH negative type and Glenn a positive, I was advised not to even attempt another pregnancy for at least ten years, fifteen would be even better. Under such restrictions, I was of little use to my husband. My mother of yesteryear, sober and caring, came to Salmon to take care of me in the early days following my dismissal from the hospital. She later told me that my features had been so distorted, bloated from the toxic uremia that she hadn't recognized me when she first arrived.

In a photograph taken days later, I, too, barely recognized myself.

Later, Glenn packed up our things, and myself, and drove us back to Sidney where I would be staying.

With all the moving about that we did (eleven times in those first two years) my memories are pretty hazy and the ones I have aren't very gentle.

The three major decision making memories were first, being left in a parked car at the curb in front of an American Legion bar in Plentywood, Montana. An hour and a half was long enough. I went into the bar, pulled up a stool and listened in on the alcohol

Phyllis Demarecaux

enlightened conversation going on between my husband and another drinking man.

When the drivel had become completely senseless, I made a remark. The stranger (to me) stopped and said, "Who the hell are you?" When Glenn didn't say anything, I said, "His wife", then turned to Glenn and said, "I think it's time to leave."

The second memory also took place in a bar. I think we were living in Cut Bank, Montana at the time. I was employed as a nurses aide at the local hospital. Glenn was, as usual, absorbed by the insights of his drinking buddies. I wandered into an attached dance hall where a jute box was thumping out its wares. One of the men at the nearby booth got up, apparently sober and bored with his company, followed me in and asked if I would like to dance.

Would I!

He was a good dancer. I don't know how long, nor how many records had spun their magic when Glenn came peaking into the room. He was not a happy camper. I suppose it seemed to him that I was enjoying myself too much. He took me by the arm, twisted it painfully behind my back and suggested in a teeth-gritting tone that it was perhaps time we go home.

It was the first time he had become physical with me, except, of course, for his version of demonstrating sexual connubial bliss.

Days later we were on our way to my younger sister, Sharon, and her husband's home outside Williston, North Dakota. Glenn was dropping me off. I would be staying with them until I heard from him. He and the high line crew were on their way to somewhere in the neighborhood of Hot Springs, Montana. There was purportedly no place there for us to live.

The reunion with Sharon was a joyful one. We laughed and hugged our great pleasure at seeing each other again. When we calmed down, I turned to offer my help unloading the car.

Glenn wasn't behind me. I stepped back outside.

He was gone.

The Color of Dusk

He'd dumped everything on the steps leading from the garage into the house and taken off without so much as a wave good-by. And that was the third memory. I took a temporary job in a small drive-in restaurant and on the better weather days, served the outside patrons on roller skates. Three or four months later, not having heard from him I contacted an attorney in Sidney who hired someone to locate my husband and serve the papers.

Glenn was a no-show and the divorce was granted in absentia. Two years had passed since our son's death.

In retrospect: Glenn's sexual education probably came from other uninformed kids of his own age. With no parental guidance there was no understanding. Having grown up with divorced parents, an absent, lascivious, uncaring father (I'd spent an exhausting two days when he visited trying to keep him out of arm's reach.) and a mother who actually confessed to me that she was afraid of her own son, his behavior and treatment of me was predictably no worse, if not better, than could have been expected.

There was no way I was going to remain in Sidney. Move back in with my parents! Out of the question. What I needed now was time to heal and what better place to choose than one where all the physical needs of life would be supplied gratuitously.

Two weeks later I was in Butte, Montana enlisting in the Women's Army Corps. I didn't pass the physical the first time, although the doctor swore to the enlisting Sergeant that I was "strong as a horse". At five feet nine inches they wanted more weight on my bones, I went back home, ate three heavy meals a day, dozens of bananas and nuts, drank a glass of heavy cream twice a day and at least eight glasses of water. Two weeks and a gained half pound later I was back in Butte and ready to go.

As nearly as I can recall, I left with two changes of clothing. The Army would be supplying me with the rest of whatever they required so I wouldn't be needing a thing. My monthly pay would be enough to cover small expenses, and of course, the payment I was making to the lawyer who had handled my divorce.

Yes, I had gotten my divorce on the installment plan.

CHAPTER FIVE

When the plane landed in Richmond, Virginia, I dutifully made my way to the local bus station where I was to pick up a ride to Fort Lee.

I was about to enter the station when somebody behind me grabbed my collar and yanked me backward, hard enough that I lost my footing. Fortunately I fell into my attacker who was steadier on his feet than I.

He appeared to be in greater shock than I. What is that about, I wanted to know.

"You're going through the wrong door," he croaked.

"Wrong door?"

"Yes," He pointed to the overhead sign: COLORED. The door next to it read: WHITES ONLY. My introduction to 1953 democracy of the South.

The doors were about two feet apart. Easy to make a "mistake" even though, once inside everyone wound up in the same space! Should I have told him my mother was Cherokee? Would he have rushed to wash his hands?

Inside that space a young black soldier who had witnessed my "rescue" informed me that the afternoon was ahead of us, that he had a three day pass and that he could show me around the city. I smiled and explained to him that I had joined the Army and was on my way to Fort Lee.

The Color of Dusk

He said that it would be weeks before I 'd have another chance to visit the city and assured me that it would be time enough if I checked in before the evening meal. He made good sense, besides, he was already a soldier so he should know.

We had a pleasant lunch in a local bistro, a brief tour of neighborhood homes, a city park and a museum after which he returned me to the bus station. I thanked him for a nice tour and a delicious lunch. It had been daylight when the bus dropped me off. It was early dusk by the time I made it, on foot, to the far side of Fort Lee which was where the WAC basic training area was located.

You're in the Army now, I told myself as I stepped into the arrival hall, the checking in station or whatever they called it.

"We've been expecting you all day," a Sergeant told me as she lead me into the barracks. "You took your time."

My response: "Umm."

"Pick any bed you like," she said, swinging the door open. "Spaces won't be assigned until everyone gets here." And she was gone.

Three or four curious recruits looked up, but only one of them volunteered to help. "My name's Claudia," she said. "Claudia Liggs." She was about my age and height, 5'9", bigger boned and slightly heavier than I, blue eyed and blonde. Her accent put her in the Mid-West. "I can help you make up the bed," she offered. "I've already been here two days."

"Just tell me how things work," I suggested and began making up the bed. She watched me silently, then, when I cornered the sheets, she smiled. "That's how they told us to do it. Where did you learn that"

"In a hospital…"

A loud bugle call interrupted our conversation.

"That'll be the supper call," Claudia announced. "We have to line up outside…. Come. I'll show you."

Outside it was a rush. We stood side by side and raised our arms to make certain we were standing an arm's length from the person

53

Phyllis Demarecaux

on either side of us. A drill Sergeant stepped out in front and called, "Attention."

Arms dropped in unison.

"Right face."

Everyone turned,

"Forward march," she barked and we were off to form another line at the Mess Hall.

Roll call came after dinner. Several platoons, including the one I was standing in, broke into song. "Down by the Riverside". The sound of our voices filled the autumn night with a sort of rich melancholy. The weather was gentle, the mood soothing. The day ended with Taps.

We ran, walked, double-timed, crawled, and did gymnastics, at least an hour every day. We learned to march and some of us, like myself, volunteered to be part of a close order drill team. It wasn't dancing, but it did require timing, and I thoroughly enjoyed myself. Claudia, before many days, became "Jiggs". I cannot for the life of me remember why. Maybe because her hair was so oily. In spite of an early morning shampoo, it was separating into spiky little twigs by mid-afternoon. Another recruit in our platoon, Alexia Gordon from D.C., became "George" because Martha was taken and sometimes, for no reason at all, we called her Able. Lookado kept her own name because it was so peppy and unique.

George, Jiggs and myself (Filly) became inseparable in-so-far as the military life would allow. We were of three entirely different natures. George actually had an emotional cry when her parents arrived a few minutes late to pick her up for her first week-end pass. Jiggs and myself were somewhat appalled. We, of course, were not expecting anyone to show up for us. Jigg's only sister was happily married and lived, I believe, in the Detroit area. Her widowed mother still lived in the little "Poke and Plum" town (poke yer head round the corner and yer plum outa town) where Jiggs had grown up. Probably, according to Jiggs, still playing "pillar of the church."

54

The Color of Dusk

The most memorable event during basic training was the day both George and myself had gone in on sick call. We returned to the barracks where we'd been confined for the day, each of us with three APC tablets and a two ounce bottle of codeine. APCs to kill the headache and codeine to drug us into submission, my friend observed.

We were in the latrine taking pills. I took mine and watched George fumbling a glass of water, the codeine bottle in one hand, bottle cap and pills in the other. She was attempting to put the extra pills back into the bottle.

One fell into the sink. Bottle, bottle cap and glass of water were placed on the shelf over the sink and she went after the straying APC. It fell into the drain opening. George went after it.

"Leave it there, George," I counseled. "The army will replace it if you run short."

"My finger's stuck," she said.

"Able." I was without sympathy. "Take your finger out of the sink."

"I can't. It's stuck."

I must have hesitated.

"Please," she begged. "Call the Sergeant. My finger is stuck."

I went to the squawk box and called the C.O.'s office.

The Sergeant's voice squawked over the squawk box. "What's the trouble, Private Johnson?"

It's Private Gordon, Sergeant. Her finger is stuck in the sink."

"Tell her to take her finger out of the sink."

"She can't take it out, Sergeant."

Silence on the other end.

"It's hurting her. It's stuck." I add.

"Is her finger really stuck?" A note of doubtful incredulity was perceptible in the Sergeant's voice.

"Yes. Affirmative. It's stuck."

"Yes, what?" It was the barracks Corporal.

"Yes, Sergeant Holstein."

55

Phyllis Demarecaux

"Yes, what?"

"Yes, Mam. Private Gordon assures me her finger is really stuck."

"…If this is a joke…. I heard her say to someone before the squawk box disconnected.

Back to Able in the latrine, I was feeling pretty helpless.

"It's starting to swell, I think, and it's hurting me."

"I'm awfully sorry you got your finger caught in the sink, Able. Would you like me to get you a chair?"

"I don't want to be comfortable. I want my finger back," she fretted.

"What's taking them so long? My finger hurts…Go see if they're coming."

Back at the other end of the barrack I was in time to see a stern faced single parade coming across the reveille grounds. The barracks Corporal., the Sergeant and the Company Commander. The CO was swinging a monkey wrench. Somehow it didn't go with the suit she was wearing, even if she was a soldier.

They stepped inside.

"Where is she, Private Johnson?" the Corporal asked.

At this point, I think I raised an eyebrow. "In the latrine," I told her.

"In the latrine," the Company Commander echoed.

"I'm in here, Mam," George's voice resounded from the other end of the barrack. "In the latrine."

"What kind of ridiculous story is this, Private Gordon?" the Commander asked as we entered the latrine.

"My finger's stuck," George replied.

"How did this happen, Private Gordon?"

"I dropped my pills."

"I dropped my pills, Mam," the Corporal corrected.

"I dropped my pills, Mam," Able repeated.

"You could have left them there, Private. Pills do not plug sinks."

"You're absolutely right of course, Mam."

"Does it hurt, Private Gordon?"

The Color of Dusk

"Yes, Mam. It does."

A brief, albeit confused, conference decided the first step would be to dismantle the sink.

One wrench of the monkey wrench and George all but howled. "This doesn't seem to be working."

I was getting tired of standing and felt that Able must be, too.

"Would you like me to bring you a chair, Able?" I asked again.

"No." She sounded pretty grumpy.

"Your friend is only trying to help."

"A chair cannot help me, Mam."

Able was being polite with superior officers in spite of her pain.

"You may have to wait awhile, Private Gordon."

"You mean they won't come right away, Mam?" George was beginning to panic.

The Corporal was back. "They're not coming at all. The post Fire Department is on its way."

A burly male Sergeant arrived at our barracks, saluted our Company Commander and asked. "What seems to be the trouble, Mam?"

"One of the trainees has her finger stuck in the sink.?" Our CO's embarrassment was evident.

The Sergeant suppressed a smile. "Very well, Mam, we'll see what we can do about it." He turned to me.

"Where is she?"

Where would he expect her to be? In bed?

"She's in the latrine, Sergeant."

"Thanks." he smirked in my direction.

An inspection of the plumbing showed that nothing could be done with the drain opening until the sink was removed from the wall. One of the Sergeant's 'boys' was sent to shut off the water supply.

Following that it was a quick job getting the sink detached, albeit with Able's growing finger still firmly imprisoned in the opening.

57

From there it was a matter of chipping and chiseling away the enamel around the opening…a painfully slow process owing to the impeding presence of George's index. But finally, three long hours after Able's not so able chase after an illusive pill, which had long since dissolved, her finger was freed.

A week later Company A's barrack, second platoon, of the ancient WAC quarters at Camp Lee, Virginia, had one modern, spankin' fired new sink. The story of Private Gordon's plight may well be one that is still making the rounds.

It was on a weekend afternoon when a group of us was playing cards in the barracks. We were seated on "Lookado's" bed when one of the barrack's Sergeants came in and screamed at us. We were never again to be caught sitting on anyone's bed except our own. Sitting on another person's bed was not allowed.

The following week the barrack's Sergeant screamed at me for not being attentive when in formation. She had me go to the end of the line at chow time in order to separate me from standing next to Jiggs. This separation went on as ordered until one day, all those people who were normally in line between Jiggs and myself, were off on Mess Hall duty. We were pleased to find ourselves next to each other but the Sergeant was not amused. Again she sent me to the end of the line, not to our platoon line this time, but to the back of the line of the platoon behind our own. By the time my turn came it was too late to be served because my platoon was already heading out.

Sometime near the end of Basic Training, Jiggs and I found ourselves in a PX in the main area of the Post. That is to say, a PX frequented by the masculine military as well as the women stationed at Fort Lee. As I recall, we were in uniform, although we would have been allowed to go in "civies". Another young woman, not in uniform, turned up. She was perhaps five to six years our senior and as we were the only other women visible, asked if she might share our table. Of course she could. She began conversation by asking if we were new to the army how we liked it, etc. and of course, we recounted all the weird behavior of our barracks Sergeant.

The Color of Dusk

Jiggs went directly to the Pentagon when our assignments came through. George was on her way to being a Chaplin's assistant at the Presidio in San Francisco and I was on my way to study control panel wiring for the IBM Machine Records Unit in Indianapolis, Indiana. We were a class of forty, thirty-eight men and two women. I've never forgotten about those miserable 2,220 jack-plug holes for the IBM calculator.

It was a surprise to run into one of the barrack's Sergeants from Fort Lee. (Not the one who had behaved so strangely.) She'd been "transferred" was all the information she gave when I inquired about it. Obviously she was not happy with the change.

There were in all, about fifty WACS in the barracks. The Post male military population was around six thousand. The mess hall was set up in two sections. The WACS were always seated at the first rows on the left hand side of the dining room. It seemed to have become an unspoken law. The WAC presence was divided. One week in the first section of the Mess hall. One week in the second section of the Mess hall. Back and forth. Who says the army isn't sexist?

However, when the classes broke for chow time, we girls were on our own. Possibly one to five hundred men would be in line in front of me and another hundred behind me before the next WAC showed up.

As I recall I accepted only one invitation to dinner while in Indianapolis. He was a Sergeant in charge of the Mess Halls, at least one of them, or something like that. It wasn't until we were seated at a restaurant table, some twenty miles from the base, when he reached across the table and took my hand that I noticed the ring on is finger.

I was still an innocent. "You're married!"

"Yes. Does it make a difference?"

"It does."

He was gentleman enough to drive me back to the barracks, but not enough to pay for a dinner. I went to bed hungry and I think I prayed to God to give me a better brain or at least to help me use the one I had. Somehow, following that fiasco, I found my Mess

59

Phyllis Demarecaux

hall duty time doubling. The work wasn't really bad. I preferred cleaning the trays and silverware as it came in and in no time at all, I discovered that I could sing my heart out and nobody would order me to shut up. So that's what I did to pass those hours. singing next to dancing was my favorite past time. Some of the work staff even joined in on occasion.

And ultimately the Sergeant in question issued me an apology.

From school I was sent someplace in New Jersey where I spent two days, then on to First Army Headquarters Fort Jay on Governor's Island. The day I was in line to check onto the base, there was a young Corporal, Joseph Adrian Moore, standing in the PIO (Public Information Office) at the end of this very long room in which I was standing. His office had just recently been redecorated, and heralded a large window wall which looked out over the entire room beyond. My glance caught his, and minutes later I was a being hustled out of the building on a TDY which he explained to me was temporary duty, and into an Army sedan. We were on our way into Manhattan. I was to be in a USO movie they were shooting with General Omar Bradley.

The General was a kind, gentle man. Hard for me to imagine him in a battle, war situation. I don't think he was certain if I was a model/actress as was the other young woman, or was I really in the Army? There wasn't a great deal of time for socializing, so if he wasn't sure by the time we finished up the day, he may never have found out.

It took Corporal Joe, along with his commanding officer, WAC Lieutenant Anita Cox, approximately two and half months to get me a permanent transfer from the Machine Records Unit to the Post Information office. The Machine Records Unit wouldn't miss my expertise. After having given me all that electrical wiring training, they had put me behind a typewriter punching holes in the IBM cards which were used in those days. I was, after all, a girl before I was a soldier. I wasn't sorry to quit the little office they'd locked us up in. The girl who worked in there with me had unbelievable body

60

The Color of Dusk

odor. The boys called her, "Perfume Patty". I hadn't been around long enough to find out if it was due to a health problem or if she was simply unwashed. Later, because of odor complaints in the barracks, they opened her locker. We all knew from whence the smell came.

The Post Information Office was a great place to be. There were many perks available to all the military, men and women, enlisted and officers on the Island that would have passed by unnoticed had I still been working in the Machine Records Unit. The General's yacht was a good example. I don't know much about its length, but it was large enough to require two life boats, each sporting a 50 horsepower outboard motor.

Not unlike a pilot who is required to have a certain number of flight hours per month, the crew of this boat was required to have a minimum number of active work hours. Joe and Ron Levy, the other man in the office, were good at helping them out. During the warm summer months, and not wanting to appear greedy, they signed for the boat only about every third week. Whether or not we got to use it, depended, of course, on the General's schedule but apparently he wasn't much of a sailor.

We went as far as Jones' Beach where we dropped anchor and the guys swam. I watched. (Traumatized by our brother's death, neither myself nor my sisters, have been able to overcome a fear of water.) Occasionally the group actually swam all the way to shore to "make time with the girls". I never asked if they told them to whom the boat belonged. They were having too good a time. Once docked back at Governor's Island we were required to write our observations and comments in the ship's log book. As a simple Private, I was outranked by most of them, but they didn't seem to think that it mattered. My entries were always positive commendations, the boat was run by a much esteemed, capable, efficient and well-mannered crew. They were especially capable the one time a guest ran the boat back a couple of yards and ended up getting the anchor line tied up in the propeller. They and the perpetrator took turns diving for close to an hour to rectify the error but it was Private Marty who saved our buns.

CHAPTER SIX

WAC Lieutenant Anita Cox was a wonderful help to us and unafraid of letting her staff try new things. This office was good training for Joe especially as he was looking to become a PR man in civilian life. I was put in charge of tours of the Island and the old Fort Jay. Our tourists were primarily student groups, young and old. It was fun and entertaining. A little research about the Island gave the tour some flair. The old Fort Jay with it's moat was always a good starting place.

Things were pretty calm in the office with Lieutenant Cox gone on a few weeks TDY (temporary duty). Corporal Joseph Adrian Moore, our non-com (non-commissioned) in charge, was, in fact, downright bored but with Dior making big news in the world of fashion it didn't take him long to come up with an idea. It's culmination began with a trip to Brooks' Costumes. There, after much hemming and hawing, he selected, a white beaded, 1920's style dress with lots of swinging strands, a clutch hat, a pair of high heels and a foot long cigarette holder, all to be worn by yours truly.

Next day, WAC Sergeant Beverly Riemann and myself were escorted into the Plaza in Manhattan. We were, we were told, to have lunch with Arlene Francis. Ms. Francis hosted a weekly live television show called *"Soldier's Parade."* Our small group also included a young private, Russell Gritsch, sitting behind the wheel of a 1923 L-Car convertible. He owned the car and anywhere it went, he went.

The Color of Dusk

Ms. Francis, it turned out, was having lunch with someone else so we waited. Joe shrugged. It would be a photo op, even if we didn't get to eat.

The photographer who'd been sent from the New York News took a few photos while we were waiting and more when Arlene showed up. The photo they printed in the News was without Ms. Francis. It carried a caption saying that "Phyliss hopes the Dior fashion will click." The picture showed me wearing Joe's 1920 selection and Beverly in dress uniform. A group of gentlemen on the street ogling us made up the background. (One of those gentlemen turned out to be my future husband.) The misspelling of my name in the picture caption was from Joe. He thought Phyliss with a single "I" and a double "s" looked more interesting.

The return trip to Governor's Island was memorable. We took the convertible down Fifth Avenue. Joe had me sit up on the back of the seat and wave my cigarette holder to the masses as we passed by. New York City streets are always heavily peopled. We were having such a good time it became contagious. Everyone was laughing, smiling and waving. The policeman at the intersection of fifth and 43rd stopped the cross town traffic and waved us on. By then, I was laughing so hard my jaws were sore and my stomach ached.

Our arrival on the Post did not go unnoticed. The Colonel, whose name I cannot remember, beckoned me into his office. I was, of course, still "out of uniform".

My 1920 dress showed a lot of knee. I clicked and tinkled my way up to his desk stopped and snapped to attention. The forgotten cigarette holder quickly changed hands. "Private Johnson reporting, Sir." I saluted.

The Colonel looked up, acknowledged my salute and with a wave of his hand asked, "What exactly does this represent?"

"Well, Sir. A designer named Dior is attempting to revolutionize the women's fashion. Not just here but throughout the world. This isn't exactly a protest but many of us are concerned as to what the new WAC uniforms will look like."

Phyllis Demarecaux

"I see," he said, with an uncomprehending glint in his eye. "But not everyone has your legs, Private Johnson."

"Sir?" *Had I heard him right?*

"Dismissed."

"Yes, Sir. Thank you, Sir."

Another awkward salute and I floundered myself out of there.

The photos with Arlene Francis were sent to the Great Falls Tribune in Montana and were published in their Sunday magazine section. Ms. Francis was pacified.

In spite of the snafu (situation normal, all fouled up) Joe saw to it that I became an extra on the weekly Arlene Francis television show, *Soldier's Parade*, at least twice a month. A young dancer, Mike Deminico, took me in hand and we ended up doing a specialty number for the show. In a part of it, I did the Charleston. Those were live audience days and in this case, audiences made up primarily of the military. It was a great feeling when the fellows all began clapping their hands and singing out "Go! Go! Go!"

A week or so later the director of the Army choir, asked me to walk past the guys and smile at them mischievously as they sang "Oh You Beautiful Doll". When Ms. Francis came in she put an immediate stop to it. She was the beautiful doll. It startled me. How could a woman as well known, as successful as she, be so insecure?

Somehow I got onto the television lists as a possible contestant and ended up winning a few hundred dollars. One of the shows actually booked me when I was home on leave. They called me at my parents home, did a short interview and scheduled me upon my return. The show was *You Bet Your Life*. Groucho Marx was the MC. I remember telling him, during the contestant interview, that the WACS barracks on Governor's Island were separated from the men's barracks by a three foot wall, referring, of course, to its thickness. Marx asked me if the guys found it difficult to jump over.

Another show was *Name That Tune*. Myself and a group of many other potential contestants, were invited to participate in a musical quiz approximately three weeks before we actually appeared on the

The Color of Dusk

show. It's one I won't forget because just as I was about to go on, one of the show's producers whispered in my ear, "The third or fourth song is *Donkey's Serenade.* You didn't get it in the quiz." I didn't think I was nervous, but when the third song struck the second note I rang the bell. *"Donkey Serenade,"* I said as the strains of *Everything I Have Is Yours* died away.

The irony was that my dance with Mike Dominico a few weeks earlier on the *Soldiers Parade* show was in part, to the tune of *Donkey's Serenade.* The fellow who had wanted to do me a favor would have done us both a favor if he had kept his mouth shut.

A week end pass and I was off to DC to visit friend Jiggs at the Pentagon. She gave me a tour of the incredibly impressive building and tried, uselessly, to help me understand how people found their way around the place. Secretly, she carried a floor plan in her pocket, because she said, there was always a possibility of making a wrong turn and, because the halls all looked alike, confusion could lead to extreme befuddlement. Our time together was too short but we continued to correspond.

Back at Fort Jay Joe introduced me to Robert (Bob) Elkon, a civilian friend of his who had been discharged just shortly before I arrived on the Island. I'm not certain what Bob was doing for sustenance when we were dating. He was heavily into the arts and my visits to the local museums were far more interesting when they were with him. Later he opened an independent art gallery on upper Madison in Manhattan. Our dates were to become regularly infrequent over the years. We enjoyed each other's company. I also dated a young GI named Allan who introduced me to my future second husband, Jacques Demarecaux.

Jacques began calling me every day. At work. One way of getting my attention, but not the kind of attention he was after. He took me out to dinner a couple of times then asked me to dinner at his parents home which I soon learned, was also his home, as was many good, unmarried sons in those days. I was immediately seduced by his family, his French mother, Andree, with her charming accent and his

Phyllis Demarecaux

blue eyed Ukraine born stepfather, Vincent, who was wonderfully literate but who mispronounced almost everything. They began inviting me regularly for weekends. I loved spending time with them and even accompanied them up-state for a weekend visit to their daughter, Tatiana, who was at summer camp.

I continued seeing Jacques on a fairly regular basis, but was not sleeping with him, which may or may not have been the norm in those days. Whatever the norm, premarital sex, or maybe sex at all, was not for me. The occasional dinner with Bob Elkon was still a given; on one occasion I dined with the Sergeant from the photo lab. He had gone out of his way to find a spectacular seafood restaurant that would be a delicious surprise to one of those "inlanders". Unfortunately I had never felt deprived living so far from fresh seafood and very definitely was not a fan. It was evident to the Sergeant that I wasn't going to make it. Fortunately he had a good appetite and was able to finish both my and his plate. He was appalled when I told him that my parents enjoyed eating fried oysters. He had never heard of such a thing.

We had a good time sharing background stories and the evening ended on a much better note than it began, but he never asked me out to dinner again.

Jacques began asking me to marry him. I told him marriage was out of the question, as was sex. He nevertheless declared his everlasting, undying love for me. I cautioned him against extravagant proclamations. "You're setting yourself up for a lifetime guilt trip," I told him. I was in the army and intended to stay there. He didn't care. I could stay in the army. It eventuality came to my telling him that we had to stop seeing each other. "But," he said. "You promised my mother you'd spend the weekend with them. You have to come."

At Andree's request, I timed my arrival for lunch. She opened the door with a flourish. The apartment was filled with people, all staring at me. "Congratulations!" they chorused. "Congratulations!" I was dumb struck, shocked, astonished and definitely speechless.

The Color of Dusk

Andree was too excited to notice. She handed me a boxed orchard corsage. "Take it….Take it out," she prompted. I opened the box, removed the flowers and dropped the box onto the sofa next to me. She pinned the corsage to my lapel.

At that moment Monsieur Floriot crossed the room carrying an enormous cake which read, "Congratulations Phyllis and Jacques. Appy engagement!" he said, losing the silent, unpronounceable h. (For the French) I think he actually bowed.

Andree, beside, me, was digging frantically into the corsage box which I had thrown aside. She fished out a small jewelry box and handed it to me. I was numb and must have looked pretty stupid. "Open it," she said, opening it as she spoke. "It's your ring." She picked it from the case and slipped it onto my finger.

Where was Jacques hiding while all this was going on? I don't remember, but he was not making himself very visible!

Most of the people present were French born friends of his parents, people I had never met. Some of their names were (and please forgive my spelling) Monsieur Etchicopar who owned a small restaurant on the island, and was a part time composer of classical music, Monsieur and Madame Fortier; he was Jacques' God Father, and a retired musician from the New York Philharmonic (as had been Jacques' father before his early death from pneumonia) and Suzanne and Gilbert Tilliard. She was a high fashion clothing designer. Her *non de plum* was Suzanne Augustine; he was a fabric designer. Monsieur Floriot, who had baked the incredible, beautifully decorated cake, was Pastry Chef at the Waldorf Astoria. Mike Elliot, of Elliot, Unger and Elliot, a television commercial production company.

Jacques' employer, Larry Taylor, Jacques' American born buddy and his sister, Tanya (Tatiana) who was the youngest person there, next to myself. There were others, but only these stand out in my memory.

It was a festive, delicious meal. Jacques' step-father was involved in luxury food imports so there was plenty of *fois-gras* and caviar.

67

Jacques had by now made an appearance and we cut the cake much as would a couple at a wedding banquet. They were a charming group, filled with the pleasure of seeing each other and of sharing our 'bliss'. In spite of my initial shock and the party's implications, I had a good time.

Next day was spent helping Andree with the clean-up. I smiled a lot. Who wouldn't? She and Vincent seemed so blissfully happy about the engagement. Several months later I was to learn, from Jacques, that his parents had expected me to pay for at least half the expense of that party and were somewhat shocked that I hadn't made the offer.

I was shocked, too. Their party. Their friends.

Jacques didn't own a car so I was up early Monday morning to get back to the base. I went on a packed rush hour subway to the end of the line and picked up the Governor's Island Ferry in time to get into the PIO office just as Ron and Joe were arriving.

"Wow!" I said. "I deserve to be Miss Subways after this morning's hassle."

Joe leapt to the occasion as Lieutenant Cox smiled her appreciation. "Of course you do! I'll set up an appointment today."

And he did. A sedan took us into town where I was interviewed and photographed. Joe, at the PIO office, would be notified as to their decision.

My behavior with Jacques is still a mystery to me. Maybe it was because of my great fondness for his parents. In comparison to my own family life, they were ideal. I loved being with them, watching them enter-act.

An even greater mystery was why did Jacques go along with it? There was nothing romantic about our relationship, at least not from my point of view. We had simply become friends. Jacques, however, did not see it that way and continued to pressure me. I ended up telling him he would have to set the date and make all the arrangements. It was my intention to continue in the Army until my enlistment was up. I don't remember what time of the year the

The Color of Dusk

"engagement" party took place, but imagine that the wedding was soon after because Jacques said he wanted it done before I had a chance to change my mind.

Ron Levy and Joe in the Post Information Office, saw to it that our engagement was announced in the New York press and with the help of Lieutenant Cox, organized a wedding shower for us on the General's yacht. They made a real occasion of it, and although I wasn't a beer drinker, they had somehow finagled permission to bring some on board. They hadn't overdone it. Two six packs as I recall, which covered one each for the male guests.

We were married by a Justice of the Peace in a little office somewhere on Long Island on the 10th of December, just two days before my birthday. Jacques' step father, Vincent Krenine, was one of the witnesses. The other was probably the Justice's wife. Jacques found and rented a one bedroom apartment in Sunnyside in the same complex where his parents were living.

I moved off the post almost immediately. A couple of the girls in the barracks were ecstatic. I was freeing up a much desired corner room.

The Miss Subways posters showed up in the metro cars in January 1955. I'd forgotten about it. Had they contacted Joe? Had he simply forgotten to tell me? Whatever. Mrs. Demarecaux was now Miss Subways. One of the gossip columnists picked up on it. Regardless of her snotty little remark, no one seemed to pay any attention. The 'honor' of having been chosen came with perfect timing for the Subway itself. They were introducing new wagons to the system and I was selected to go along with them as a new and satisfied subway traveler. Most of the New York papers covered the story at one time or another. (New York had five major newspapers in those days: *The Journal American, the New York News, the Mirror, The New York Post and the New York Times.*)

A *New York Times* photographer came to the Island the 21st of January and took a picture of me walking the "ice covered rails of Governor's Island". I was sincerely pleased and flattered but probably

Phyllis Demarecaux

didn't appreciate how exceptional it was for the *Times* to run the photo of a nobody on the front page.

I don't recall exactly when, but someone had written a documentary of the island. The photo department decided to put it to film and I, the tour guide for visitors to the Island, was selected to 'reinvent' myself on film. The Sergeant - director, who was in charge did an excellent job. It was later shown on a local television station. I was introduced following the film and quizzed about my life in the Army. That interview was completely relaxed. On the other hand when the WAC Captain enlisted myself and a couple other girls to participate in a live lunch time fashion show at the Waldorf Astoria, it was another story. I was petrified. It took place at a luncheon she was attending at the Waldorf. I remember her, the Captain, coaxing me to smile. It didn't happen.

Joe even managed to get the press involved when my discharge came through. The *Daily News* photographer had wanted me riding the Ferry with discharge in hand. They ran the picture in the center fold and headlined it "WACS Lose Face." It was flattering and funny.

I used my discharge money to purchase an MG for Jacques. He had never owned a car. Not unusual for people living in a city where public transportation was so abundant and affordable. It was, however, a shock to me when Andree, my mother-in-law, told me with glee what a pleasure it would be not to have to take the morning subway ride anymore. I expected Jacques would clarify things for her, but he didn't. Result was, he left our apartment every morning, stopped in his mother's place for a morning coffee and the two of them zipped off to Manhattan in my gift.

I took the subway. Work was in the Times building in Times Square, the only building in the 50's featuring same day headlines in a continuous neon banner which circled the building. The company in which I worked specialized in supplying written material and/or photographs to the nation's House organs.

Two memorable subway incidents come to mind.

The Color of Dusk

A male friend and neighbor from Sunnyside and myself were in the train, on our way to work. It was crowd packed morning rush hour and we were, deep in conversation, clutching the pole in front of us for balance. Suddenly a woman standing next to us gave my friend a resounding slap on the face. Our eyes swept to her in shocked surprise. My friend's left hand still clutching the pole, let go with his right and rubbed his cheek lightly. "Madame," he said in a quietly, calm voice, "You have insulted not only my morals, but my taste."

Would that I could think that fast.

My second subway memory I was seated. Again the train was jammed with the rush to home. The very fashionable Burberry raincoat on the gentleman standing in front of me was open and revealed an equally fashionable blue suit, handkerchief carefully tucked in the upper jacket pocket and a Windsor knotted necktie. His left hand clutched the overhead bar. His right dropped to his fly, my eye level, and carefully unzipped his trousers and began fishing. With his raincoat falling in a straight line on either side, I quickly realized I would be the only witness to what he had in mind.

It had been a long day. I had no intention of giving up my seat, I'd worked too hard to get it. The warm flush of embarrassment for what was happening saved me.

"Sir," I announced loudly and clearly, "Your fly is open."

He was gone so fast I didn't even see which direction he took. A few curious eyes looked my way, a woman who'd been standing beside him acknowledged understanding with sparkling eyes, a grin and an approving dip of her head. I returned her smile, took out my book and read until we came to my home station, Sunnyside.

Ron Levy, also discharged, soon became a member of our staff. A free lance writer, Art Whitman, hired on a temporary job was impressed with some of my work and when he left for another permanent job, talked his new employer into hiring me. The new employer was a magazine packager. I wrote all kinds of nonsense for a pocket sized magazine which featured, among other things, young

Phyllis Demarecaux

starlet wanna-be types. The photographs gave the girls' names, measurements, hair and eye color, sometimes height and hobbies. From this I wrote three or four hundred flattering words about the girl's sparkling personality, her social talents, her ability to shine even on a cloudy day or perhaps her fight to climb unattainable heights, to become an inspiration to her family and to be the deciding factor in the rapid ascent of her family from poverty to prosperity.

Not everything I wrote was about pinups There was a magazine format story book on the life of Edgar Cayce and another on Card Game Rules. We also worked as packagers, put *True Detective Stories* together and worked with *Coronet* magazine.

Following my brief stint as a journalist, I became at my husband's suggestion, a fashion model. I reported to the Huntington Hartford Agency. They lined me up with a number of photographers who were happy to help me get a photo book together and I was on my way.

A young man at the agency asked me if I would be interested in playing Jane Eyre in the new West Coast theatre they were opening. I declined. Was it a serious offer? I doubt it. That kind of thing was often just a pickup for the uninitiated. A way to get into a lady's knickers. I do know that the West Coast theatre did open with Jane Eyre and an actress named Martha (Hyer?) played the roll. She was, I believe, Huntington Hartford's wife.

I had a similar offer while working in the Little Shop in Macy's. The Little Shop was where designer clothing was sold, Dior, Channel, Nina Ricci, etc. The offer was a seven year movie contract. Propositions come in all sizes. What would the contract involve? With exactly what studio? We could talk about it over dinner.

I voted for a nice dinner at home with my husband. I'd read between the lines about seven year contracts and even, as a model, had been offered a weekend on Errol Flynn's yacht. Women were supposed to be flattered and some probably were. I knew better and sex, in spite of this second marriage, was not a priority in my life.

Pamela Garaway, wife of David, the man of 'peace', produced a documentary about nurses' aides. She hired Jacques to do the

The Color of Dusk

filming and myself as the nurses' aide. It was a short half-hour film. We wrapped in less than a month. Jacques did a good job. He had an excellent eye and had worked as a free lance photographer before being hired by the Elliot brothers. Unknown to him, his mother had used 'politics' to get him the job with the Elliots. She was from the old French school. A steady paying job was better than working "hit and miss" of the self-employed. To her way of thinking she was offering him a security he wouldn't necessarily have as a free lancer. Maybe she was right. Maybe.

The modeling business was not particularly rewarding. There were the purely photographic jobs. I walked in, sat down on a stool and did a slow 360 turn while the camera flashed away. That would be it, they said. I stood up. They thanked me, I thanked them and left. Live fashion shows were definitely more interesting because the fashions themselves, were interesting. I recall one near disaster in particular.

Dressers behind the wings help the models into the clothes in which they are about to strut down the isle. One woman holds the dress in front of you, you step into it. She zips it up as another places your shoes at your feet and you step into them. Still another hands you the accessories, should there be any, and you're on. In this particular case, there was an additional move. There was a cape. An unseen woman threw it over the dress from behind and another hooked it in the front. "What kind of hook?" I questioned frantically. No time to receive an answer. I was on. I did my strut and about halfway down the isle, attempted to remove the cape. I tried lifting the hook, pulling it backward, forward, upward and downward.

It would not separate.

The proud designer/announcer, as frustrated as I and probably livid with rage, suggested I pull it off over my head, which I did with a flourish. There was a round of applause. Because the dress was a bare back, I did the expected turn round about and felt a pop. The long bra I was wearing had unsnapped and folded under itself right

Phyllis Demarecaux

down to a single hook at my waist which was holding the entire outfit in place. I literally ran off the runway, down the stairs and into the backstage room. It wasn't my last show, but I never worked for him again.

Television jobs were few and far between. I did a couple of jobs for Jacques employers, the Elliot brothers, Steve and Mike. They had purchased one of the first video tape machines. The tape was much wider than that which was ultimately used in your everyday VCR machines. I was the unpaid model they photographed in their first efforts. That was fun.

You have to like a job to be good at it. You have to get some satisfaction from your work. There has to be a feeling of accomplishment. Something. Be it tangible or intangible. For me it was the finale of the last fashion show that I did that made me decide to quit the modeling business.

We were a roomful of girls dressed in richly colored, heavily frilled cocktail wear, and in my case, with an equally frilled, large brimmed, matching hat. My outfit was an outstanding shade of luscious burgundy. The dress whispered as I walked. I was enjoying the feel of it when I spotted another girl across the crowded room. I hadn't noticed her before. Something about her drew my attention in a way that none of the other girls had. She seemed more interested in what was going on around her than she was in herself. I began slowly working my through the crowd toward her, trying not to be too obvious. I glanced, unobtrusively, in her direction. I was getting closer. Another girl spoke to me, I turned and acknowledged her presence, then looked back toward my objective, took a cautious step forward, then another. I stopped. Shocked.

It was a mirror and the girl was myself!

CHAPTER SEVEN

Back to work for Art Whitman. Aside from his free lance writing, he and a buddy were attempting to publish a magazine of their own. Things didn't work out and six months or so later I was again, unemployed.

Meanwhile a French friend, new to our country, was very much in need of someone to care for her infant child. I'd been helping with her English and she'd found a job as a waitress at a restaurant in the then Idlewild International airport (today's Kennedy). They needed the money more than Jacques and myself needed my own income so I quite happily became their baby sitter. By now I had aborted a couple of times and it didn't look as though I would ever be able to have a child.

So Armelle came into our lives. I stopped working, stayed home, cared for Armelle, painted the apartment and took cooking lessons from my French mother-in-law. Armelle was walking. Talking wasn't her thing. Not yet. Too many switches in language. French at home and English with me. She began calling me "Mamma." Her mother became "Mamma Therese". She sat up at the table with me when we had lunch and was proud to be feeding herself. Like all children, she understood a great deal more than she was able to verbalize.

She had been with us for the better part of one year when her parents divorced. Her mother, Therese, feeling unable to properly care for Armelle on the income she was getting, chose to send her

Phyllis Demarecaux

daughter to France where her parents, Armelle's grandparents, would take care of her. It was a heartbreaker.

The memory of standing on the stairway in our apartment building as her mother took her away is as vivid as yesterday. Therese was holding her hand. Armelle stopped and looked back at me. It was a sad look, as though she was asking for help but not getting it. She had somehow understood that this good-bye was not like the others. It was permanent.

Jacques and I decided to get a dog. We bought a female Collie and Jacques named her Smirnoff. Smirnoff because she drank most of the drink he had sitting on the step beside him the day we made the purchase. The others thought it was funny to see the poor puppy floundering helplessly around in circles. I was not amused.

Smirnoff turned out to be a good companion. It was she who, on one evening stroll, alerted me, that there was someone hiding under the tunnel cover on our parked MG. I took her back to the house and suggested to Jacques that he have a look. Smirnoff had been right. The would-be thief was frightened out of his skull at having been discovered. Jacques gave him a sermon then let him go with a warning to leave the neighborhood and do it immediately. From there, Jacques wandered over to the neighborhood bar for a quick shot of vodka where who should he run into but the still shaken potential thief. He slid off the bar stool, threw a couple bills on the counter and left.

Jacques spent three hours the next day reconnecting the wires which had been pulled from beneath the dash board. He was probably regretting having let the guy go.

Weekends were most often spent on the schooner Escasoni owned by Torbin Jonhke. Torbin's brother, along with actor-producer Mark Miller, was also part of the regular weekend crew. I wasn't much of a sailor but did well as a galley cook. The boat was berthed at the Larchmont Yacht Club. From there, we'd set up a *rendezvous* for the dinner hour meeting place with other weekenders. It was usually a full day trip. Once arrived at the destination, we'd drop anchor and

The Color of Dusk

tie onto each other. Then the guys would boat hop, sniffing for the perfume of a better dinner. I've a great memory of David Niven dining on the Escasoni. He said it was the pungent odor of garlic that led him to us. Everybody else seemed to be into sandwiches.

By now Jacques was doing a lot of "late work", most of it at the bar in a 54th street French restaurant called the *Brittany*. There were, of course, some lady friends involved. He had always been a moderate drinker, but unlike my mother he was the good natured cloud nine type. Initially I hadn't realized just how far he was beyond the occasional drink. Once I became aware of his addiction I tried to make certain that he ate, regardless of what time he showed up at home. Food would help keep the DTs away.

While we rarely raised our voices if ever, at each other, neither one of us was enchanted with our life together. Toward the end of the summer I scheduled a short visit to the family in Montana. I needed to see my sisters and, of course, baby brother, Michael, who was fast growing up. Aware that, since Armelle, I was being financially supported by Jacques, I chose the least expensive, Greyhound bus route.

While changing buses in Chicago I met David, a fellow traveler who was to become an unforgettable person in my life. He was on his way to Alaska. When the bus arrived in Glendive, Montana, where I was making another change, we debated stopping over for the night. It would be wanton, but it could be wonderful. But we didn't. We exchanged addresses instead, and promised each other that we would write. I gave him my New York address and he gave me his in the Carolinas. He went on to Alaska and I ended up in Sidney, Montana.

During the visit in Montana, I managed to convince my sister, Jane, to come visit New York City. "You never know what's going to happen in life," I told her, "and I'd love for you to see the city. Ask for a leave of absence. Do it while you have the chance."

"I can't," she said. "I've only been working there for three months."

Phyllis Demarecaux

"If you don't ask," I told her, "We'll know that you can't. So ask!"

She was granted a full month's leave of absence and we Grey-hounded our way back to the city.

The apartment was empty when we arrived but music was playing and all the lights were on. It was a bit early for Jacques' night cap so I assumed he was visiting his mother. The kitchen sink was piled high with unwashed dishes. No automatics in those days and Jacques wasn't about to do a "woman's work".

Jane and I were well into the dishes when he cane in smelling of "courage" and a need to "speak" to me. It was urgent "Sure". I threw the dish towel across my shoulder and followed him to our bedroom. He sat down on the bed. I sat down beside him.

He took a deep breath.

"I'm in love with another woman. I don't know what to do about it."

I don't think I was even surprised. "Well," I said. "The first thing you do is divorce me."

His expression was one of uncomprehending astonishment.

He protested.

"But, she's married, too."

"That," I said, "is your problem."

I left him sitting there, went back to the kitchen to finish the dishes and to explain to Jane what was happening.

She slept in the guest bedroom that night. I slept on the living room sofa and Jacques slept in the master bedroom. He left for work the next morning without breakfast. Perhaps he wasn't quite up to facing me while sober.

About ten o'clock I called a lawyer friend of ours, Bernard Katz, told him Jacques would be calling about a divorce and suggested that I did not want him to be discouraged.

Jacques called me about 11 am. "You called Bernie."

"Yes, I thought we'd probably need a lawyer."

"You weren't wasting any time."

"There's no need to let this kind of thing drag out."

The Color of Dusk

He was home at an unusually early hour. It had been so long since I'd seen him home before eight or nine o'clock I'd forgotten what the actual closing time was at EUE (the Elliot, Unger and Elliot studio). I suggested he invite his parents over so he could break the news. He wanted me to explain to them. I refused. It was his show. He should tell them.

He began speaking French as was their custom, but I stopped him when I discerned what I thought was some far-out harrumphing in his explanation.

"Tell the truth, Jacques."

He was shocked. His parents were surprised.

I didn't speak French but I was good at reading tone and meaning and I knew Jacques well enough to know when he was lying. I also had four years of hearing the language spoken around me and I'd studied French in a USAFI course while in the Army. I would have had to be totally spaced out not to pick up a minimum of the language.

We managed to get things straightened out. It was agreed that I would be staying, temporarily, with his parents. At least until the divorce was final. Jane would be staying with my old army buddy and friend, Jiggs, who was now living in Manhattan on the Hudson River side of the city. At the time, New York state law recognized only adultery as a grounds for divorce so like many others, I flew the divorce express to Juarez, Mexico.

The idea brought out my penchant for writing poems.

> *I don't he s e z, and I flew to Juarez.*
> *Life is like a hula hoop. In 20 days I flew the coop.*
> *You may not believe this but it's a fact*
> *very few people are caught in the act.*

Things went smoothly in Mexico in spite of the fact that I'd forgotten to take my passport with me. When a half dozen (at least) passengers identified me as a passenger on the early divorce express

Phyllis Demarecaux

from New York, the pilot gave the go-ahead and I was on my way home.

Back in New York, I moved in with Armelle's mother and her friend. Jane thanked me for a good, unexpectedly interesting time and bused back to Sidney.

Jacques was out of my life. I took a temporary job at the book store in the East Terminal at Idlewild airport.

I wasn't sure what I was looking for. Confirmation perhaps. I knew that my lack of interest in the physical aspect of a relationship was on the lowest end of the totem pole. David, the man I'd met on my trip to Montana, a complete stranger, was the first man I'd ever met who elicited a totally new and unbeknown reaction on my part. I needed to know if I was normal and somehow felt that he was the answer.

I contacted him, my Greyhound bus acquaintance, who was now back in Carolina. He jumped on a plane and met me at the book shop in the Eastern building where I was working. Two husbands later. It was a first for me. The weekend we spent together was, for me a revelation. We exchanged letters almost daily when I returned to New York and until I flew down for our second and last weekend together. The "Good-bye" was painful for both of us, I think.

Three or four months prior to the divorce, Jacques's mother had gone to Paris to visit family. She'd wanted me to go with her, but Jacques had adamantly refused. He did not want me turned loose among all those Frenchmen without him at my side. Well, now the picture had changed.

Therese suggested that a job in France could get me medical attention which would help me have the baby that my American doctors had said was so very unlikely. My resolve was strengthened by Isaiah 54.

The more I thought about it, the more I told myself I should go to Paris. A twice recurring dream made the decision for me.

The Color of Dusk

> *I was walking toward an open door in the sky. It
> was some distance beyond me and just slightly to my
> right. Should I walk through it?*
>
> *There was no need. It was in the sky. I could walk
> around it. But if I walk around it, what purpose
> would it have served?*
>
> *I walked through without closing it behind me
> and never looked back.*

When a marriage goes wrong it's not because you cook badly or that you don't dress well. It's not because you don't keep the house clean or make your bed in the morning. It's not even because he/she snores or reads newspapers in bed while you're trying to sleep. It's lack of communication and always a deep feeling, at least from my point of view, of personal failure.

I did, thanks to David, know that the principal, if not the only reason for the failure of my marriages, was my indifferent response to their sexual overtures. Had I met David earlier, or perhaps later, in my life, everything would have been different. We could quite possibly have built a loving friendship, a lifetime relationship. I can only imagine that we would have been happy. We did sustain a correspondence for several years. But the timing was wrong.

I've often thought of him over the years and prayed that his marriage was a successful, rewarding, lifetime adventure.

I made arrangements for passage on the *Liberte*. Armelle's mother, Therese, would be accompanying me. We were both anxious to see her daughter. We met only two passengers with whom we remained in touch. One of them was Gerald, a student on his way to Leeds, England. The other was "George", an American who taught English at Berlitz.

Following our arrival at LeHavre, we took the boat-train into Paris. Therese had arranged for our temporary stay in the city. It was a small apartment belonging to her parents whose primary residence was in Besancon. Her father manufactured wristwatches. They had

Phyllis Demarecaux

arranged for the use of a maid's room for me, *17 rue Theodule Ribot,* a stone's throw from the *Parc de Courcelles* and a hop, skip and jump from the *Arc de Triomphe.* Therese and I visited my new future landlords, Doctor and Mrs. Frederic Lemann, who showed me the room in question.

It was on the 7th floor and could be reached by way of the service entrance which led to a separate circular stairway at the rear of the building. The deal was that I pay for the work necessary to make the place habitable, plastering and painting in exchange for the right to live there rent free. I would also pay my own electricity. We shook hands and I uttered my first words in French. *Merci. Merci infiniment.*

Therese put me in touch with a painter who said it would take him two weeks to get the job done. We shook hands and I once again, muttered my good-bye in French. *Merci. Merci beaucoup.*

The waiting-for-the-room time was devoted in part to a quick trip with Therese to Besancon to visit her parents and my beloved Armelle.

They were seated at the lunch table when we arrived. Armelle, somewhat to my shock, was being spoon fed by her grandmother. She definitely remembered me and I could swear she was ashamed of being such a 'baby' in my presence. She had been so proud of being able to sit at my table and feed herself. But she was in another world now. I attempted to reassure her with a smile of encouragement.

Seeing Armelle is probably what validated the fantasy I'd dreamed up while on the boat-train coming to Paris. Should I try to have a baby? It was still a thought worth hanging onto.

Within a very few days I bid good-bye to Therese and family. The maid's room wouldn't be ready but I was anxious to check out the painters's progress. Anxious to get started with my new, solitary life.

Only one other passenger was occupying the train compartment on the trip back to Paris. We eventually exchanged names. He, Hans, would also be looking for a place to stay in Paris. There was

The Color of Dusk

some kind of major convention going on and hotel rooms would be at a premium, I mentioned the possible helpfulness of the American Express office, so, back in Paris, at his request, we shared a taxi. The American Express office was, as advertised, able to do a search. A small hotel near the *Gare de l" Est* was their answer to both our prayers.

We arrived at the hotel together. He checked in first. My ear for the language wasn't good enough to pick up exactly what information was being exchanged between my train acquaintance and the hotel clerk, but her reaction gave me the feeling she was reading more into my relationship with Hans than met the eye.

After checking in I left for the day, haunting the department stores for furniture in the children's department. Why children's? Because a room, approximately nine by fifteen feet, could quickly become dwarfed with oversized pieces of furniture. My bed, of course, had to be a standard length. The rare space beside it would be filled with a small night table which embraced a couple smaller tables and would serve multiple purposes. A chest of drawers completed the bedroom area.

Cooking would be done on a two burner kerosene camp stove perched on an upended footlocker sitting next to the sink. For the moment it housed a couple tennis rackets and a pair of Picasso reproductions.

The long wide slope on the wall to the left, the result of a chimney for the fireplace in the adjoining room, would become a bookcase with shelves built in by my handyman painter.

Small was adequate for most things, but the dining/working table would have to be full height. Tenacious searching produced a table with fold down sides, but not so far down as to prevent slipping my one adult-sized chair under its wing. The ensemble fit quite snugly under the sill of the only window in the room. I could do my typing there and when necessary, liberate the space by putting the Royal Standard typewriter on the bookshelf to my left.

Phyllis Demarecaux

A small lamp for the bedside table, a discreet fixture for the overhead light, a towel bar next to the sink (cold water only) and ten days later the room, smelling of fresh paint and gleaming in the whiteness of it, was announced habitable.

The building Concierge had already proven her value by overseeing the arrival of my purchases and seeing that they were properly delivered to number thirteen, the room I would be calling home.

The room was ready, but I wasn't. Hans, my train companion, had borrowed money for medical purposes and was now saying that he must leave for Geneva. He did not have the cash to reimburse me, but his Parisian friend, Bernard Huffer, owed him money and would be happy to take care of me. He had called Bernard, he said, and made the necessary arrangement. He left me with a telephone number and a handshake.

I pocketed the phone number and prepared to leave the hotel.

Another surprise! My generosity had left me short of cash. There wasn't enough to take care of my hotel bill. My bank account was still in New York City so it was going to take a few days to replenish my pocketbook. A bank passbook in those days had to accompany any request for a withdrawal. I filled out the necessary papers, air mailed them and the book to the New York Bank. My remaining cash in hand went for the purchase of a loaf of bread and a box of dried prunes. The bread lasted four days. The prunes lasted much longer. I savored them and kept the pits soaked in water. It was surprising how much flavor they created.

Small town hick that I was, it took me three days to discover that the price of my still unpaid hotel room included a morning *petit dejeuner*, (breakfast) so my eight day fast wasn't as bad as it sounds.

My bank book with the requested withdrawal authorization arrived on a Saturday. Monday morning I made my way, on foot, to the Parisian branch, sucking prune pits and spitting them with enthusiasm, one by one, to the curb. Banks normally open on Mondays, so imagine my consternation when I found the doors

The Color of Dusk

closed. A kind lady on the street who witnessed my dismay informed me that it was a bank holiday. They would be back to doing business as usual on Tuesday. I regretted my haste in dispensing with the prune pits and once again reminded myself that one must never assume. The remainder of the day was spent, drinking a great deal of water, reading and napping.

Tuesday morning I treated myself to a *cafe' au lait, croissant* in the Hotel breakfast room, then made my way to the bank.

Money in hand I stopped at a nearby *Bistro* and ordered a succulent, richly endowed plate of old fashioned Sauerkraut which came with steamed potatoes, a slice of ham and a wiener, all saturated in the flavor of whole grain black pepper. The ham and wiener I could do without, but the sauerkraut..! I could not stop smiling. My meal also came with a carafe of house red wine. (The house red wine in France is part of the fixed price menu or was in the 60's. Other drinks such as milk, coffee or tea are extra.)

Back at the hotel I made the call to Han's friend, Bernard. To my surprise, he offered to drive over to the hotel and haul the baggage and myself to my new home address. I packed my bag, dragged it down to the check-out desk and paid my bill. It wasn't long before Mr. Huffer drove up in a white Mercedes sedan, a big car for Paris streets.

He knew nothing about owing money to Hans. Hans owed him. Him and apparently a number of others. According to Bernard, he'd left Besancon owing a considerable amount to one of the major hotels. There had been other unpaid charges involved. With the police looking for Hans, he told me he wanted to get me out of the hotel before they showed up. It was, he suggested that, under pressure, Hans would be capable of attempting to implicate me.

Once ensconced in my new maid's room. I had to claim the remainder of my baggage from the *Liberte* which was in storage. Beyond thirty days they would begin to charge me. I showed up with hours to spare.

Phyllis Demarecaux

The steamer trunk was not going to make it up the seven flights. With the Concierge's permission it could be stored in a shed in the walkway leading toward the service stairwell, and was.

Bernard kept in touch and, knowing I wasn't in the best of conditions financially, hired me to help with the distribution of books, the *Serie Noir,* to the city *Kiosks.* It was a once a month thing and lasted about four days.

I took new titles to the *Kiosk* and picked up the unsold titles from the previous month. Occasionally there was a tip but the most I recall getting from a single stand, was the equivalent of five cents. The publishing house paid me about 0.75 cents a day and Bernard paid for my lunch.

The editor for whom we delivered those books asked if I would like to earn more by typing a manuscript which would run about three hundred pages. I accepted knowing that in spite of the challenge, my French vocabulary would be greatly advanced with such a project.

At the time, manuscripts in France were often hand written. Should the editor feel that a story merited publishing, it was he who paid to have it typed. I don't recall the name of the novel, just that there was a great deal of *brume* (fog) involved. I purchased a dictionary, for about half of what I was paid, to do the job and eventually wore it to a frazzle. The manuscript turned out to be 340 pages. Astonishing as it seemed they told me they'd found only two typos. One of them I recall was the word *peche.* The e takes a circumflex. Silly as it sounds, the *peche* (fish) wear a chapeau (the circumflex) but the *pecheurs* (fisherman) does not.

CHAPTER EIGHT

Early evening window shopping climaxed when my attention was drawn to a half dozen people in front of a store window display. Curiosity peaked, I moved in closer to get a better glimpse and found myself staring at the televised face of my ex-husband's uncle, journalist, Frederick Pottecher. His mellifluous voice was pouring out news on the French/Algerian situation. I'd met him in New York City when he was covering the tenth anniversary of NATO. I questioned the wisdom of giving him a call so soon, but succumbed. His response to my call was "Please tell me you are not the bearer of bad news." I assured him that I was not, told him I was in Paris and asked if there was any chance of seeing him. "But of course," he declared. "Immediately." Then gallantly, "It is always valuable to be seen with a beautiful woman."

It was good to see his familiar busy browed, clean-shaven face. He took me to a *bistro* on the *Ile Saint Louis* in the *Place Dauphine* where he was greeted with genuine enthusiasm. I attempted to tell him in my limited French how proud I was to be lunching with such an important journalist. He begged me to stop. He was, he said, my uncle and an admirer and he wanted to know more about what had happened in my life.

I gave him the short version. Another woman. Divorce. When he asked me how I felt about it, I confessed it wasn't the divorce that was bothering me, it was the deep sense of personal failure. When I asked about him, he was a widower and had been for a number of years, he was reticent, but said he was thinking of marriage to a lady friend who was in his life.

"Does she know what you're thinking?" I asked.

He laughed outright and said that he would tell her about it one day.

From the direction our conversation went, I surmised that he felt he was doing too much traveling to ask for his lady friend's hand in marriage. She would be finding herself at home alone a great deal of the time.

She's alone now, too, I wanted to say, and without the assurance that you will return to her. But I didn't. It was none of my business.

I was intrigued, but did not attempt to learn where his assignments were taking him. As a foreigner I felt I shouldn't meddle in the country's politics. The current political atmosphere in France with the Algerian crisis was explosive. The country was very tense.

Nervous streets, armored military trucks and armed policemen were everywhere. Frederic's muteness on the subject of his work was, presumably related to his desire not to lose connections imperative to a journalist. I was uncertain as to whether or not he agreed with the government's handling of the situation. As I understood it, radio and television news reporting in France was very much controlled by the government in power. (Almost certainly no more than in the States, in spite of what we Americans like to think.) In any case it seemed to me there was very little pro Algerian propaganda irregardless of the huge number of Algerians who had fought for France in World War II.

Meanwhile Frederic loved his work and stood fast to his convictions.

By the time we'd finished lunch he'd loaned me a key to his apartment. I would not take advantage of the broader offer of actually using the apartment in his absence, but I most certainly would take advantage of the guest bathroom - if the lady in his life didn't object - and he assured me she would not.

The Color of Dusk

It was time for him to get back to the trial he was currently covering. We hugged. No pats on the back, just a long warm hug. I thanked him again for his understanding and for the keys to his home. I would no longer have to disrupt the Lehman's home life with my bathing habits.

On a separate front, I pulled out one of my children's stories and tried peddling them to a publishing house which, I had learned through the Chamber of Commerce, was partially owned by Americans. The 'Boss' wasn't in. His secretary turned out to be Corinne de Longevialle, a French girl who had been educated by nuns in a Catholic school while living in what then was the British East Africa Protectorate. (It wasn't until my 35th birthday, December 12th, 1963, that the now independent country became Kenya.)

She was sympathetic to my cause and promised an early reply. We made a coffee date. I was to learn that Corinne was the good Samaritan. She was always ready to help people who found themselves in positions such as myself. Also, she enjoyed pleasing her father, a man who, she said, liked pretty girls and her mother didn't seem to mind. It wasn't long before she invited me to dinner in their home. We were destined to become close friends. She reported that the boss liked my Wiggle Worm story but it wasn't the style of books published for children in France. Illustrations had to be realistic and my Wiggle Worm certainly wasn't.

It was time to begin the classes for which I had registered at the *Alliance Francaise*. They were great. I'd never seen such a diversified mass of serious single-minded students in pursuit of knowledge. Turbans, saris, jackboots, tie-vested suits, skirts and jeans represented a multi-colored, paisley rainbow. Our inability to communicate in a common language was a great class leveler. The teacher, a petite genius, was a package of dynamic energy faced with a formidable task. She spoke to us only in French, using short, full sentences, occasionally doing line drawings on the blackboard, always gesturing with hands, eyes, eyebrows, fingers, arms, feet and legs when necessary to get her meaning across.

Phyllis Demarecaux

Repetition served us well. By the end of the day we were able to give our name, address and nationality in a completely correct, full French sentence. By the end of the second day I was able to tell my fellow classmates that I took the *Metro* to school each morning, which in those early "prune" days was really not the case. I had walked.

I became an avid reader of French articles on medicine and psychology because they were loaded with recognizable words. Technical terms were often spelled exactly the same in English. Only the pronunciation changed. These books on familiar subjects were to become my greatest exercise in reading aloud. In less than a week we were discussing the weather.

By then I'd become friendly with a stunning, graceful reed-slender brunette named Inga. Having always assumed the Swedish were blonde, I was surprised to learn she was from Stockholm. Her English was first rate.

When I complimented her on it, she told me that people spoke English in Sweden because it is a small country. "What does size of the country have to do with speaking English?" I puzzled.

"How would we communicate with the world if we spoke only Swedish?"

A point well taken.

Speaking English in class was not pleasing our instructor, but having someone with whom to communicate beyond wild gestures and pointing fingers was a great cure for loneliness.

We were into the third week of school before I learned the French name for the circular stairway which led up to my maid's room. It was a stairway *en calimacon*.

Inga volunteered to help me unload the steamer trunk. Did she know that I lived in a 7th floor walk-up? Not exactly but she knew I lived in a maid's room and that access was by a stairwell, so the chances are she understood the folly of her undertaking. Between the two of us, it took eight trips to unload the contents of the trunk which sat in the Concierge's shed on the street level.

The Color of Dusk

Out of breath, hungry and near exhaustion we sat in my little room contemplating the mass of 'stuff' I had brought with me from the States.

The typewriter was already there, of course. Now came a Singer sewing machine, books, framed art for my walls, a guitar and two tennis rackets.

Why two?

I brought the extra racket for an eventual game partner, in the event I found one. In the face of reality, the whole idea was now moot as Therese had explained to me. Many French people did not play tennis. In part, she said because most clubs required white dress and membership fees were costly.

Inga seemed surprised that I had so little money. She'd always thought that Americans were quite rich. Rich and romantic, she said. It was because of the movies. We all seemed to live in nice homes, had a family car, ate very well and sang songs which spoke mostly on love, either of each other or of our country.

Our friendly and romantic image of the past is long gone. The bulk of American movies today are made up of special effects, war, murder, blood, robbery, greed, speed, drugs, sex, alcohol, nudity and hate. Certainly not much to inspire confidence and nothing to sing about.

My reward to Inga for her help was an invitation to the movies. We settled in to watch singer, actor Ives Montand, in the original version of *Les Salaries de la Peur*. (The Wages of Fear) The story is about three men who are hired to transport trucks loaded with nitroglycerin across the desert. It was like watching a silent movie. We understood the story but not the words.

The house lights went on and a lady with a basket laden bouquet of ice cream and candy came down the isle selling her wares. We treated ourselves to chocolate bars and sat back to watch the film again.

The second time we understood more and having understood more, began to realize how little we understood. We were far less

Phyllis Demarecaux

satisfied with ourselves than we had been after the first time around but the system was working for us.

We actually sat in that theatre from two in the afternoon until ten o'clock that night. What a wonderful way to make progress.

Inga was working as an *aupair* for a French family with three little girls and didn't have as much free time as I, so I bravely returned to the theatre the next afternoon on my own, this time with a couple of sandwiches hidden in my pocketbook. It was another long day at the movies but I was beginning to separate phrases into individual words. In all, I spent about sixteen hours watching that movie and today I have it on video in my home entertainment closet.

About that time my landlords, Doctor Frederick Lehman and wife, Francoise, invited me to a delectable dinner party at their home. Francoise was a stunning size twelve with an appealing, unstudied simplicity. While she submitted an occasional question, she left the bulk of the discussion to her two friends. We were a group of five.

Marie Helene produced an educational program in conjunction with the ORTF (*Office de Radio/Television Francoise).* Her show done extemporaneously, would unfortunately be out of the question for me, she said, but she would like to see me when my language skills could handle talking without conversational lapses. A dynamic, voluptuous young lady of mature proportions, she lit cigarettes with cigarettes leaving a gray blotch of ash in every chair she occupied, both before and after dinner. She wore a brightly colored sheath with an unexpected flare to the skirt. Regardless of the opinion she was presenting she appeared agitated. Jumping from her chair, her skirt swirling around her, she would circle the room in search of words each time she spoke. It was a remarkable delivery. Whatever she was saying had to leave her listeners, if not convinced, impressed. I understood very little of it.

Danielle, the second woman, was a handsome gray-haired youngish grandmother with a Lauren Bacall body. Dressed in a long jacketed, grey suit with a snow-white blouse, she presented a sterling calm next to the agitated movements of Marie Helene. She remained

The Color of Dusk

seated while speaking and spoke with the quiet dignity of one who, though not accustomed to having her authority questioned, was completely open to being questioned. She was a physicist. Attached to France's atomic energy program, she worked in the Administration of a plant about forty kilometers outside Paris. She did not talk shop.

They were heavily into a political discussion. I was able to contribute the information that I was, or had been, before the divorce, a niece of Frederic Pottecher. They were impressed but their questions about him were on a personal level rather than about his political leanings. I told them that I found him to be a quick wit with a sense of humor, irony and I especially appreciated the enthusiasm he held for the work which he did. I'd been witness to the recording of two separate broadcasts. A shorter one for the earlier version, a second for the more detailed, later program.

My French was still very limited, but I was already understanding far more than I was able to speak. When asked what I had been doing with myself, I told them about my marathon at the movies. Suddenly, I recalled a word which had been used fairly frequently and I had not been able to understand its meaning. The word was *con*. My limited knowledge of latin/greek prefixes, etc simply told me that it meant "with". It was, however, evident even to a non French speaking viewer, that "with" was not what it meant in the movie. I blurted out my question. What was the meaning of the word? There was a quiet, stunned silence.

Ultimately, my doctor landlord suggested that his wife might discuss its meaning in more detail at a more appropriate time. For the moment, he said, it meant "with".

The difference between French and American women, their jobs and their attitude toward their jobs, was startling. In a country where a married woman could not have a bank account without her husband's permission, women were holding positions about which American women only dreamed. Even the head of the Council of Europe was a woman. French women seemed to have learned

Phyllis Demarecaux

the secret. They did not attempt to be sexually competitive, only professionally competitive. There is a difference.

I thoroughly enjoyed the evening although I left feeling inadequate. They were more knowledgeable, more at home with their lives and far better educated than I. No multiple choices. You either knew the answer or you didn't. Their twelve year "Bac" was the equivalent of two years of college in the US. It was more diversified and more educational, certainly in part because there were no competitive sports attached to the school system. Competitive games, basketball, soccer, tennis were played after school and were not considered a part of the curriculum.

My first invitation to a major French party came by way of Corinne de Longevialle. It was the celebration of the birth of an encyclopedia for children which would be published in *fascicules* sold weekly at the *kiosks*.

(newsstands) A first in France, it was called *Tout L 'Univers.*

Corinne picked me up in her *Simca Mille Fiat.* The party was to take place at the *Palais de Chaillot* in the *Place du Trocadero.*

She was dressed in multiple layers of sheer silk of contrasting pastels ending at the cocktail length. The bodice crisscrossed around her neck and fell from her shoulders in sweeping lengths of flowing fabric.

She hadn't mentioned dress. Not that I could have done any better. She noticed my assessment of her wardrobe and indicated that the party was not fancy, just exclusive and by invitation only.

"Your invitation is in my handbag," she said.

Was I dressy enough for the occasion? I was wearing a red Treina/ Norrel knit with a close around the neck top and three-quarter length hip to shoulder raglan sleeves. Simple but elegant. My former mother-in-law, Andree Krenine, had worked as assistant manager in the Manhattan based home where these dresses were made. Individually hand cut and, in my case, made to order. It was a part of my wardrobe, a four or five hundred dollar dress, an intriguing contrast with my living quarters.

The Color of Dusk

Corinne pulled to a stop light and gave me a knowledgeable once over. "You're perfect," she told me. "Women will be jealous and the men will be reeling. Relax and let Paris do the work."

I thanked her. It was a relief to pass muster in the world's fashion capital.

Traffic in the *Place du Trolcadero* seemed horrendous but Corinne quickly found a parking space.

People were crowded around the entrance to the *Palais,* apparently out of curiosity as few seemed to be entering. Inside we stepped onto a brilliant red carpet where even the commonplace was approached from a different point of view.

The full length of the brilliantly red-carpeted stairwell was lined on either side by spectacularly uniformed young men in razor-edged black trousers with red hip-length jackets trimmed with gold braid and buttons and wearing highly polished, gleaming black shoes. All this blended to perfection by high, fluffy black crown, patent leather billed hats trimmed with glittering gold, punctuated by tall red pompons.

They were, Corinne told me, members of the French *Grade Republicaine* in charge of the security of the President. Its members, she explained, could be engaged as Honor Guards for special occasions.

This was one of those occasions. The French really know how to throw a party.

Each guard snapped to attention as we walked past. We followed the red carpet up a luxuriously wide stairway unlike any I had ever seen outside the movies.

A crier, also uniformed, black trousers, red tailed coat, took our invitations at the landing. He stepped into a reception room shrouded by a huge vaulted ceiling and announced our arrival in a full booming basso.

Mademoiselle Corinne de Longevialle.

Madame Phyllis de Marecaux.

Phyllis Demarecaux

A second uniformed aid handed each of us a cone-shaped package of glazed almonds of the type traditionally passed out at baptisms. A huge banner at the rear of a podium set up at the far end of this gigantic hall announced the birth of the new encyclopedia: *TOUT L'UNIVERS.*

Corinne wanted me to meet her boss. Why? He had refused to publish my Wiggle Worm.

She indicated a dark, handsome, smiling man of about forty with a full head of thick, unruly hair. Early signs of pudgy tendencies peaked over the Pierre Cardin buckle at his waist and tugged at a shirt button barely bearing up under the strain. Beside him an equally handsome woman dressed in a flowing red silk print, also dark, also smiling, stood looking up at him with a combination of admiration and discomfort. Probably not as at home in this ambiance as her husband.

Having helped hostess several major New York parties for Elliot, Unger and Elliot film company I was familiar with what I believed her to be feeling. Her husband undoubtedly worked on a regular basis with at least half the people around us and used the familiar *"Tu"* when speaking with them. After awhile a wife begins to feel like an interloper and the smile freezes on her face.

"Mr. and Mrs. Beressi, I've brought you Phyllis de Marecaux," Corinne announced. Each extended a hand. I grasped and shook them in the French tradition.

"Phyllis has submitted some children's stories," Mr. Beressi said to his wife in English. "They are under consideration."

Under consideration? My ears must have flopped forward.

Madame Beressi smiled. "Shalom," she said.

I offered my thanks and hesitated, hoping to hear more about my stories, yet knowing it wasn't going to happen.

We moved on.

Corinne's cousin Francoise Guerad, early thirties, taller than Corinne was slender with an athletic build. She was an extremely

The Color of Dusk

handsome woman with the kind of sculptured good looks that get only better as time passes, leaving the beneficiary virtually ageless.

Armand Bigle, a man with a jovial round face and attitude, was perfect as head of the Walt Disney offices in France. When he learned I had written children's stories, he suggested there were occasions upon which they might have work for me. His wife was a nice looking woman with more deftly outline features than her husband and with large eloquent eyes. I remember her wearing an extremely sheik suit of burnt orange silk.

Bertrand de Vaudoyer was an exceptionally tall Frenchman, about six/four, and a journalist who did not speak English. He explained this "shortcoming" by saying he was a notoriously lazy writer.

He and Corinne had become friends during the years she worked PR for Pan American Airways at the airport's VIP lounge. They kept in touch and saw each other on dinner dates about half a dozen times annually.

The Count Francois du Bois de Riocour, another exceptionally tall Frenchman was one of Corinne's current suitors. Handsome and self-assured, with considerable charm, he brought my hand to his lips in a courtly manner, saying *"Au plalsir"* and to Corinne, *Comment va tu, ma Cherie?"*

Bartenders clothed in long-tailed dinner jackets, rushed about, their trays laden with cocktails, champagne and punch for the adventurers.

Great mounds of *hors d'oeuvres,* both hot and cold, represented every culture present and I was determined to sample as many as possible. The Greek, *feuilles de vines* were popular with everyone, I tried one, a second and still a third. The Japanese *edamame* was another favorite. Teriyaki chicken on serving sticks, colorful vegetable sticks with a selection of at least a half dozen different dips, fifteen choice cheeses with various breads and crackers, kabob of marinated lamb, beaf cooked with vegetables, onions, tomatoes and green peppers.

Phyllis Demarecaux

An enthusiastic admirer swept Corinne away before she had time to introduce me. It was stupid to have come without money, but I had, so since I was unprepared to return home alone, I kept my eye on them. In so doing I realized there was a good deal of flirtatious behavior. Nothing outrageous. Nothing tasteless. Just old fashioned flirting for the fun of it.

I hovered over the food long enough to qualify for giving recommendations to those who were uncertain about their choices. Everyone was friendly but they did not introduce themselves. Generally they were with someone or part of a group.

The subtly diminishing hum of animation led me to thinking it was time to do some scavenging. Corinne was still wandering about with her friend. I set off to rescue a few empty almond cones and as discreetly as possible, began preparing doggie bags to be secreted in my handbag.

Not quite as discreet as I had hoped. I was caught and questioned by a journalist, a younger version of Corinne's friend, Bertrand, with a glib tongue and a flirtatious tendency toward the double entendre. I plead guilty saying I had a sick friend, too sick to be able to attend the party. His response was to request one of the waiters to bag a selection of the *hors d' oeuvres* for me.

"You are very kind," I told him.

"Peut être," he said with a devilishly seductive gleam in his eyes, "We should get together privately, and discover one another. ''

"Sorry to break up the party, Jean Paul. Another time." Corinne announced over his shoulder and gave him a devilish look.

As a consolation prize she told me he would probably keep in touch with me if I had a telephone.

She also suggested I should apply for one immediately because, she said, it could take as long as two years for me to get one.

Two years!

I took her at her word and made the application.

Optimistic and with God on my side, I felt certain I'd be able to afford one in two year's time.

CHAPTER NINE

Paris rooftops fascinated me. Neat little rows of small brick-red pots seemed to be everywhere. They looked somewhat like inverted argyle planters sitting on the chimneys, one for each apartment or fireplace in the building. Apartments in older buildings were, in 1960, heated individually rather than through central heating systems and maybe still are.

The camp stove I bought was serving as much for heat as it did for cooking. When bathing, I was getting additional heat by burning off kerosene in an empty coffee tin which I placed on the floor in the middle of the room. Bernard Huffer had offered to loan me money for an electric heater. It took some convincing to keep his money in his pocket. I not only couldn't afford the heater, I couldn't afford the electric bills which would have resulted. Neither could I afford to pay off a loan. My weekly twenty-five dollar alimony checks had arrived regularly the first six months. After that, it appeared, I was on my own. With the bulk of my cash already invested in my living quarters, I did not a *gaie divorcee* make.

My early experience with the lack of cash had made an enthusiastic walker of me. I walked everywhere. An out-of-door tourist. I visited the *Louvre* Gardens with the *Arc de Trioimphe de Carousel,* the boat basin in the *Jardin des Tuilleries* and Victor Hugo's home grounds in the *Place des Voges* where uniformity of the surrounding architecture is more than it would seem at first

Phyllis Demarecaux

glance. In spite of similarities, each building carries its own separate architectural history.

I was also becoming more adventurous with the language. No more 'point' shopping. I named the product and, of course, I was venturing further away from home and asking more questions.

Street sounds were also teaching me. *"Bonjour Madame. Puis-je vous aider avec quelque chose?"* (May I help you?)

Another oddity of which I'd become aware: the French drink a lot of wine but there was very little or no mention of any social programs for alcoholism. For all their drinking reputation I had yet to run into a group of really drunken Frenchmen or women anywhere. Exuberant, happy, rarely boisterous, not even rowdy. I'd check out this impression on New Year's Eve.

Back in the 60's Paris was a woman's town. Walking down the *Champs Elysees* was a constantly changing adventure into the world of women's fashion. Were it not for the lack of women's hats, everyday could pass for an Easter parade. Yesterday's *Champs Elysees* surpassed by far, the elegance of New York's Fifth Avenue.

American influence has changed all that. Of course one can still sit on the sidewalk terrace near, more often than not, an American styled fast food set up, enjoy an *espresso* and watch a world of jeans and tee shirted pedestrians as they stream by. Americans should feel very much at home.

Paris is also a city where men love women. And Frenchmen do love women. They treat them with respect. Never condescending. Nothing macho. Interest, attentiveness and admiration. Their attitude definitely made me less conscious of myself as a person and more aware of myself as a woman. None of that "I've got to prove I'm a man" attitude. No hawking up slime and spitting on the sidewalks. This may not sound like New York, but it is most certainly familiar to those in Montana where I grew up. High school boys where I went to school were already measuring the distance they could spew their slime.

The Color of Dusk

With all the ambiguity I felt enriched just by being there. Paris came closer to being the single most important romance in my life. Beautiful, cathartic Paris.

Shops opened early in the morning so who cares if they closed between noon and three o'clock! We were all busy having lunch then. Besides, they reopened at four-thirty at the latest and most remained open until seven or eight pm.

Department stores on the Grand boulevards put up outdoor stands. Entire lengths of sidewalk were given over to merchants who attempted to out-shout each other over the worth of their wares. Multiply a single street vendor by dozens and you have some idea of the mass confusion rendered during business hours. Not even the rain stopped them. They put up umbrellas.

When the *Marches* (outdoor markets) were open it was virtually impossible for a car to get through. For all practical purposes streets were closed to traffic during those hours but why take away the picturesque, the color, the hustle bustle? Why ask the French to be practical?

I also learned that as a shopper I was expected to furnish my own basket, shopping bag or whatever, in which to carry my purchases. It took me countless trips up and down those seven flights, in a building where ceilings were ten feet high, before this very important fact finally registered with permanence in my mind.

Mother-in-law Andree had impressed upon me the countless inconveniences I was likely to encounter in Paris. She remembered well her introduction to the United States and wanted me to be aware of what I would be up against, knowing that isolation could be grueling, knowing also that there would be time for soul searching and hard work.

Weeks without a single totally satisfying, coherent conversation with another being could take its toll. Of course there was the Concierge. She chatted about the demands made upon her. I sympathized. She complimented me on my progress in French. I praised the *Alliance*, its teachers and God.

101

Phyllis Demarecaux

All this was helpful but a good conversation, even one about the weather, would have been an exciting novelty in my new life. Some days I told myself I could pack up and go back to the States. A walk through the city, becoming acquainted with its celestial majesty and the notion was quickly cast aside. Only occasionally did I allow myself to go through the litany of David and the "what ifs…"

Early morning hours I spent walking along the *Quai* of the Seine absorbing the healing melancholy of its murky message while observing the often erratic, always absorbing the behavior of the human species.

Back to the more earthly things. I discovered outdoor circular public walk-in *pissoirs* for men. Women, left to fend for themselves, often found relief by visiting the closest *Tabac*.

My late husband had told me that New York City once made a disastrous effort to furnish similar conveniences for men. They became exchange points for drug dealers and stalking points for perverts. As a result, today millions of tourists find themselves asking permission in restaurants, coffee shops, bars or hotels to avail themselves of the facilities reserved for customer use only.

One invariably found *toilettes* or WCs (water closets) as the French often called them, in an area that also housed pay telephones for public use. Privacy was questionable both for the telephone and for the toilet. It was, in fact often difficult to discern which, the telephone or the toilet, was more public.

The base of the toilet was a concrete or enamel surface approximately two and a half feet square, poured on a decline of 20 to 30degrees. Two flat parallel rises at the fore of the square clearly indicated "Place feet here and squat". Men, of course, could stand, depending upon the urgency of their visit. The slope terminated at the rear of the square in a centrally located four inch diameter hole. Some sports minded Englishman had penned his assessment of the situation on the wall in my favorite neighborhood coffee shop: A damn good putt.

The Color of Dusk

When using the public telephone one is advised to remain alert to the sound of flushing. Doing so allows time to clear the deck before getting your shoes soaked.

An early assumption had me believing that these toilets, called Turks, were available only to occupants of maid's rooms such as my own. The very limited space one had to move about had me crediting the expression "housemaid's knee" to their existence. I learned otherwise in a quick pit stop at a remodeled, up-to-date restaurant on the Champs Elysees.

Consideration given to the mandatory position for women was, in about fifty percent, a low, conveniently place handlebar which one could grasp for support. A flush chain hanging to one side, when pulled, opened the flow of water from an overhead bowl. Usually in good repair, users could squat with the assurance of drip-less comfort. Again, however, I recommend one make for the nearest exit as far as possible before flushing.

The American Express near the Opera received an incredible galaxy of people, many of whom used it as a temporary mail drop. Short term residents, students, tourists, business people, upper, lower and middle class. All nationalities. All colors. Women and a surprising number of men, unwilling to commit to the use of the *pissoirs* in the street, chose to make a pit stop before leaving the building.

Tabacs, however, were the most popular of the public systems. A purchase at the bar is not required (but appreciated) for access to the premises. Many furnish no paper. In others carefully cut rectangles of yesterday's headlines hang in prominent display. While they serve the purpose, I learned to carry tissue in my handbag. Newsprint is not the easiest stain to remove from one's knickers. When regular store-bought paper is available, one is expected to leave a tip. On rare occasions there is an attendant.

Whatever inconvenience the use of public toilet encumbers, it is far easier, in Paris, to spend a morning studying French over a cup of *espresso* in a warm cafe than to sit shivering in an unheated room

Phyllis Demarecaux

with a cold water tap. A single cup of paid for coffee (or tea) was all it took to spend two to three morning hours in the warmth of the cafe with no objection from the management. As soon as the lunch crowd started moving in, I vacated my seat. Afternoons I could usually be found back in the cafe by 3 pm.

There were other regulars as well. A group of four gentlemen met regularly each afternoon. A month or two went by before they began acknowledging my presence. The gentleman who worked at the bar noticed their interest in me and made it his business to let me know that the "gentlemen" were neighborhood pimps. He suggested they may attempt to take advantage of my innocence and he wanted me to be aware of the danger. I was grateful for his watchfulness.

Not having a telephone was probably the convenience I missed the most. My only recourse was to remain in touch by mail. In-city mail could be sent by *pneumatique* with a three hour delivery guarantee. It was, however, a service too dear for my pocketbook.

Should I send a note to Corinne de Longevialle? Would she be shocked? Americans were known for their quick familiarity. Would she think me too forward? Perhaps I should stop at her office, invite her for a cup of coffee and pray she wouldn't order anything to go with it.

The dilemma was solved one early Saturday morning when she presented herself at my door. Her parents would like to have me to dinner. Would I be available for seven o'clock?

Of course I would and the fact that I arrived empty handed did not leave them gasping in shock.

Corinne's parents had an interesting history. Her father had been CEO of a profitable Anglo/French tobacco and pineapple company in the British East Africa Protectorate since 1928. He was eventually going to be one of the few men who actually negotiated the sale of the company to a newly independent country now called Kenya. Most companies, I was told, were simply taken over by the powers that be. Her mother, a de Seze and daughter of a French ambassador, had waltzed through her teens in the world's capitals, Rome, Vienna,

104

The Color of Dusk

Rio de Janeiro, wearing ball gowns and Cinderella slippers. It was the *Belle Epoque* about which we have heard so much. Her brother, Hughes, Corinne told me, qualified as a professional tennis player. He would, however, at his father's urging, later become an Admiral in the French navy.

It was the beginning of a long friendship.

CHAPTER TEN

I'd installed myself in the *Tabac* one particular afternoon and was deep into irregular verbs when a gentleman seated at the table next to me asked if I might know where the *rue Saint Patrick* was located. My response was automatic.. *"Desolee, Monsieur."* I'd returned my attention to the books when I realized the Paris Metro Guide was laying on the table next to my portfolio. Turning to him, I indicated the guide. Navy blue suit, navy blue topcoat, blue Fedora hat, navy blue scarf, white shirt and a soft, amiable face, gentle, intelligent with unflinching eyes. Thirty/thirty-five at the most.

He moved toward me with a quick understanding smile and together we bowed our heads in search of the illusive *rue Saint Patrick*. It was several seconds before I looked up again and said with regretful finality. *Vous vous etes trompe, Monsieur. La rue Saint Patrick n'existe pas."*

"You are not French," he observed in English, his smile untroubled.

"And you, Sir," verbs temporarily forgotten, "are not lost."

"Ivan. Ivan Cesar," he replied, tipping his hat.

I immediately noticed it was covering a full head of hair.

"I am from Argentina and it is my honor to ask if you would kindly be my guest this evening for dinner and a show at the Lido. I offer a truly French evening. Not only with myself, but with a serious minded, gray-faced, French business and his charming wife both

The Color of Dusk

of whom proclaim themselves descendants of Napoleon. A truly, utterly, boring couple. Would you not like to save me?"

I must have taken a deep breath.

"You cannot possibly say no," he rushed in ahead of me. "I am a foreigner alone in the city. You, who are also alone, must certainly understand. To dine alone in the city of romance is unthinkable. Are we all destined to be spectators?"

"But you just told me you were not alone."

"Accompanied. Yes, but alone. With you at my side and the diversion of the show, they will speak their language..." Here he flashed a major smile and switched back to English... "And we shall speak yours." He stood, swept his hat off and bowed.

I was more intrigued than amused as I sat watching the show at the ringside dinner table in the Lido that evening. A little different from the New York City Roquettes. The girls, divided into two groups, either fully costumed dancers or topless mannequins, were within touching distance on a stage about elbow level from our seated position. In fact Ivan Cesar did stand, leaned over and caressed one of the girl's leg during the show. She responded like a trooper with a smile, and, to my rhythmic eye, an un-choreographed kick. An on stage waterfall and pond with swimmers was immediately followed by an ice rink. Skaters, blades flashing, swished past our table.

The champagne dinner, the show and Ivan Cesar's company were great. To end the day, that began in a cross table conversation with a young Argentine playboy, middle-aged French industrialist and His wife, was beyond anything I might have imagined. But then Paris was full of surprises, good and bad.

Writer/Producer Robert L. Joseph told me that stage director, Harold Clurman, once said he'd rather starve in Paris than eat well in New York. An exaggeration, of course, but his point was well taken. Many Americans have gone to great lengths to cling to Paris. Ex-patriots stayed on because they found it the most unique city in the world.

Phyllis Demarecaux

Ivan Cesar and I met the next day for lunch but had no time to get seriously acquainted. His plane was leaving in the afternoon for London and from there he would be flying back to Buenos Aires. We exchanged addresses and parted knowing with unspoken certainty that we would meet again.

Everyone in Paris meets again.

CHAPTER ELEVEN

    Sunday, April 9th was to be another surprising day. I'd been on the terrace of my favorite *Tabac* taking in sunshine, coffee and attempting to read Alexander Duma's *The Three Musketeers,* in French. My idea was that it would be easier to understand the French when reading a story with which I was familiar. One of the Russians from the nearby Cathedral stuck his head between the book and my face. He'd been blessed with a prominent forehead, heavily lidded, wide-set eyes, a slim lined nose, full lips on a generous mouth. Long slender fingers combed back a shock of dark semi-long hair that had fallen across one eye.

    "A beautiful day requires beautiful company," he announced in fragmented French. "You cannot possibly be reading."

    I remember looking past him to the incredibly blue sky beyond and decided he was right. What I really needed was to take advantage of the glorious weather, to take a walk. Days spent studying were too sedentary. I closed the book, laid change for the coffee and made my way off the terrace.

    He followed me. Down *rue Faubourg St. Honore.* Elegance and style. No plaster mannequins here. Clothing draped, dropped, swirled. Combinations of shapes, materials, colors. Sometimes as little as a single gown bespeaks the street's refinement. Glistening shop windows displayed glass, antiques or paintings. *Hermes. Lanvin.*

Phyllis Demarecaux

My shadow temporarily forgotten, I walked leisurely through this shoppers' paradise enjoying the intimate glimpses it gave me of still another Paris.

Faubourg St. Honore became *Saint Honore.* The quality began to dwindle, the prices a little more approachable, but not for me.

By now he was asking my nationality. Was I a painter? I had fine, sensitive hands. Was I a musician? Was I a Parisian or was I in Paris studying?

"Mmmm", my reply to all, was a conversational sound to which I'd been introduced in a letter from the Leeds student I met on the *Liberte* coming over. He'd given a vivid description of the British use of 'mmm' in conversation. It served a wonderfully diplomatic purpose. It could be used to indicate that you agreed with the speaker, that you disagreed with the speaker or as a simple acknowledgement that you were listening. Entire groups of people could be heard 'mming' as one of their chaps busily expounded theories about anything, everything or nothing. I enjoyed Jerry's letter tremendously and loved the idea of 'mmm'. This had been my first chance to put it to use.

By now we, myself and my shadow, were walking along the *Quai* of the Seine. Barges, their flat decks covered with lines of laundry flapping in the breeze as they swished quietly up river, *Bateau Mouche* boats loaded with tourists and artists sitting along the bank, easels before them, busily brushing their magic.

It was time for a coffee break. *Place de l'Alma* at the angle of Avenue *Georges V* and *Avenue Montaigne,* I chose a table in the covered area of the outdoor terrace *Chez Francis.* My Russian admirer drew back the chair next to my own, seated himself, signaled and when coffee arrived he paid the waiter. I nodded my thank you, "mmm"..

We sat quietly enjoying the day and were preparing to leave when a rain squall forced us to move into the shelter of the restaurant. Time stopped. The clatter of dishes ceased. The scene became a still life, the only movement coming from the owner of a *kisoque* just outside

The Color of Dusk

the terrace. Transfixed, we watched her scurry to rescue her very perishable merchandise. Plastic sheets appeared from nowhere and were draped over the entire stock, but left no place for the owner. She whipped a thoroughly soaked stocking cap off her head, ducked onto the terrace area joining us for cover, nodded almost apologetically, whipped a *Series Noire* paperback from her apron pocket and became engrossed in the French translation of Ian Flemming's 007.

We listened to the brisk energy of the rain squall waiting for it to ease off. It did not ease off. It merely stopped. As suddenly as it was there, it was gone. The sun reclaimed it's place in the sky. The rustle of life returned. The restaurant was back in motion.

Up the *avenue Georges V,* past luxury hotels, the *Prince de Galles* and the *Georges V* and across the street at the corner of the *Champs Elysees,* the world renowned master of cuisine art, the restaurant, *Fauchon.* Food at its finest.

I led the way toward the Arch of Triumph, located at the *Place de l' Etoile,* where twelve major avenues converge. The trip around the Arch as cars weave their way into and out of the circle can be fearfully breathtaking to a newcomer. In those days, it could be just as breathtaking as tourists made their way on foot through the traffic in order to reach the Arch where the tomb of the unknown soldier could be visited on a daily basis. There was also, as I recall, a room near the top of the Arch where photographs of its construction and history were on display. From there, one could climb to the top of the Arch and look down over the impressive 360 degree view of this magnificently planned city. The *Champs Elysees* on one side of the Arch continued on the opposite side as the *avenue de la Grande Armee.* Each one led to a view into infinity.

French President Pompidou killed that perspective on the side of the *avenue de la Grande Armee* when he allowed a series of high rise structures to be built in *Saint Cloud.* The powers that be are, however, attempting to make up for that error and a visit to the area as it is today, can be well worth while. All buildings leading up to the Arch on either side are uniform in height.

Phyllis Demarecaux

I was moving into home territory, down the *avenue Wagram*, past utility shops and restaurants, the *Cammioner* being my favorite. I crossed over to *rue Poncelet* from the *Place des Ternes,* entered a *boulangerie* and selected a *demi-bagette.* My ever present Russian was still with me and it was he who paid for my purchase. I protested with an "Mmmmm", but he insisted it gave him pleasure.

Outside, I once again, crossed *Wagram.*

Theodule Ribot. My building. I stopped and extended my hand.

He appeared to be astonished. "You mean you're not inviting me to dinner? Not even a drink?"

"Niet. Non. Nada. Rien." I said. "But it has been a very pleasant day away from my books and I thank you," I continued in English.

"English," he said. "American." He stopped. Reflected. Continued. "I will carry a fond memory of this day." He said it warmly, appearing to mean it. He extended his hand. *"Bon soir, Mademoiselle."*

"Bon soir," I said, both relieved and disappointed in myself. We shook hands and I remember watching him walk slowly up the street, his head slightly inclined.

I was, I had suddenly realized, past thirty, a two-time divorcee and an inexperienced amateur in the art of being picked up.

112

CHAPTER TWELVE

My family, including Aunt Florence, in their rare letters, never failed to ask when I was coming home. They were either concerned about my marrying a Frenchman and staying in France or worried about the French/ Algerian problem. Stories full of bombings made our day-to-day living conditions appear much more disruptive than they were for the bulk of the population. There was danger, of course, but the acts of terrorism were, for the most part, not taking place on residential streets. They were, however, sufficient to disrupt the tourist industry.

News organizations often select the exceptional which, by its very nature, leads to the exploitation of isolated incidents. The thrill of sharing fearsome, spine tingling, real life threatening situations within the confines of a safe environment, one's living room, is exciting. Thanks to television, news in the 60's was already becoming entertainment. Television "News" programs today even go so far as to announce "coming attractions" and at least one network, gives a choice of three different "newsworthy" events. The viewing audience then e-mails their choice and the winning story is featured in detail.

The city was another story. Busloads of military and tanks were strategically aligned in the principle *Places* guarding the government buildings and the people of the Elysee Palace. A city under siege waiting, eyes skyward, under the ominous threat of an invader, paratroopers trying to overthrow President de Gaulle.

Phyllis Demarecaux

Parisians came out by the thousands in the hope of witnessing the event first hand. Traffic on any given bridge was a nightmare of congestion, the atmosphere charged with excitement on the fringe of fear.

My only direct encounter with anything concerning the "Algerian problem" took place on a a late night return from the local movie. I'd just turned into *Theodule Ribot* when a man dressed in a suit, the jacket casually open, began closing the distance between us. I carefully drifted closer to the buildings and slowly, imperceptibly, increased my pace. Several steps later, realizing he was falling behind, he rushed rapidly across the sidewalk toward me. I responded quickly, lengthening my stride moving toward the open street.

"Attendez!" he called, pulling something from his pocket.

A gun?

"Arretez. Police. Je suis avec la Surete."

Without breaking stride, I turned my head and looked toward him. He was, effectively, holding a police badge at arms length. I slowed, but did not stop. *"Oui,"* I said. *"Et vous voulez?"*

"Nous cherchons deux Algerians. Do you live in the area?"

By now I'd arrived at the door leading toward the courtyard to my maid's room. "Yes," I told him.

"Be vigilante," he counseled me and added, "If you run into anyone unknown to you on the stairwell, call us."

Common sense told me if the men they were looking for were dangerous, they would check the place out before allowing me to enter.

They made no such offer. I nodded acquiescence and climbed safely to my domain.

The transit police had never bothered me, never stopped me or asked to see my papers. Although part Indian, to the average person, I am Caucasian. My darker skinned, brown eyed younger brother and sister would probably not have gotten off so easily. Because of their skin color, countless North African, Algerian citizens of

The Color of Dusk

France were obliged, both on trains and in the stations, to produce ID papers for police inspection. As in so many countries, our own included, the attitude of officials was not always as respectful as could be hoped.

Would someone throw a plastic bomb at me? I didn't think so.

Frederick, the journalist uncle, was another matter. I still had a key to his apartment and, because he was gone so much of the time, made regular visits, three times a week, to his bathing room. Choosing to limit my visits may have saved my life. Frederick had been out of town the day a bomb was planted on his doorstep. The explosion effectively destroyed the front entrance and my favorite bathroom. His reportage concerning the Algerian/French situation was certainly the reason for their discontent. Frederick's only comment was, "I've made somebody unhappy with me."

The bombing left me sufficiently shaken up to keep my mouth shut regarding my personal feelings toward the Algerian problem… Not enough to give up bathing, but enough to give up bathing in Frederick's apartment. My landlords had also given me permission to bathe in their apartment once a week so, along with visiting American friends and their hotel bathrooms I managed to remain 'fresh' in spite of my diminished living conditions. In fact, I at one time considered writing a Tourist's guide to Paris Hotel bathrooms.

I made very few friends that first year in Paris. Days were spent mostly studying the language. Thanks to Corinne, I had a small radio. It was turned on the minute I rose in the morning and remained so for as long as I was home. The idea was to surround myself with the French language at all times. I made no attempt to understand what I was hearing. It was approximately six months after I'd gotten the radio that the *Place des Ternes,* my home *metro* station was bombed. When the news hit the radio, I was shocked into realizing that for the first time, I was not just hearing the announcer, I was listening and understanding him.

And that's how children learn a language.

Phyllis Demarecaux

Aside from Corinne there was Bernard Huffer and, of course, my landlords, Francoise and her doctor husband, Frederick Lehmann. Frederick was an electric train addict. He ran nine lines set up in a room three or four times larger than the one I lived in. An intelligent, chubby man bordering on forty, it was he who spoke to me about the often inferior housing, the occasionally 'backward' ways of Parisian living. World War I had taken the lives of an entire generation of young men and put the country's growth back by thirty years. The country had recovered somewhat from World War II because as a Nazi occupied territory, their war was an underground war, in which, understandably, they had lost fewer men in battle.

Frederick's observations led me to a better understanding of a social structure and a greater appreciation of the government's efforts toward making life easier by elevating the comfort level of its people.

Conversations with someone to whom I felt I could convey an occasional coherent thought were rare, but for the most part, I continued to avoid people who spoke English. My goal was to speak French. Not wanting to get sidetracked meant I was lonely. I hadn't come to France for a life that was merely different, I'd come to prove I could make a life for myself, by myself, to recover a measure of self-esteem and perhaps, to have a baby. Once I'd been told it was very unlikely that I would ever be able to have a child, the need to do so seemed to have become stronger. That chance, however, was still a long way off. I had to learn the language, get a legal work permit and find a job.

The French were an interesting, friendly people and as a nation, were decidedly better culturally educated than an American counterpart. Lycée students, as early as the American seventh grade level, were studying Moliere, Balzac and Montaigne. They quoted Jacques Prevert and enjoyed the music of Bach, Rachmaninov, Tchaikovsky, and Mozart as well as Jacques Brel, Yves Montand, Edith Piaf, Glen Miller, Ella Fitzgerald and Harry James. They are an intellectual people. The United States is a physical country. It's about might, muscle and money.

The Color of Dusk

In spite of lonely, winter gloomy, overcast days, I was happy. And lucky. I was thirty-two years old and felt light hearted and adventurous. I awoke looking forward to each day. Looking to a future which, by the grace of God, would be bright and worthy, a feeling which left me better off than any number of the people I encountered daily.

I'd fallen in love with another aspect of Paris. The city was book ended with parks. Over two thousand landscaped acres with lakes and riding paths on the west side were known as the *Bois de Boulogne*. Drive through it, because in today's world, according to Parisians in the know, the *Bois* has become a feasting area for drugs or sex, be it professional or not, single, multiple, for pleasure, money or all of the above.

The family oriented *Bois de Vicennes* lay to the East. Leafy paths, small ponds, waterfowl and a zoo! Heights of artificial rock, bounding animals, cafes, peanut stands, children and adults basking in the sun.

The city has no Central Park for the public, but a small, medium or fairly large park can always be found within five to ten minutes walking distance from wherever you are standing. They offer a refuge, peace, contentment and security, as well as safe havens for the delightful adventurous prancing of small children, accompanied by a parent or their nannies, to be sure.

Intermittent visits from New York friends kept me from hunger. In particular Suzanne and Gilbert Tilliard, friends of my former in-laws. Suzanne was the dress designer, her husband the artist specializing in fabric design, who had been present at the surprise engagement party Jacques' parents had thrown for me. They, and others, took me out to dinner. I've dined with Louis Jourdan to my left and Lily Dache to my right. Miss Dache did not recognize me. I recognized her because I had posed for pictures, wearing one of her hats, while still in the Army. Seeing Anthony Perkins in "Good-bye Again" (*Aimez-vous Brahms?*) reminded me of a near collision with him in the revolving door of the *George V* hotel the night I

Phyllis Demarecaux

visited friends Steve Elliot and his then fashion model wife, Georgia Hamilton. I was approaching the door. Mr. Perkins hopped out of a cab and rushed toward it just as I arrived. It was probably apparent I recognized his famous face but having become accustomed to French gallantry, I did not cede my position but, to his obvious surprise, moved to the fore.

Girl friend, Jiggs, remained a faithful, as well as my primary correspondent. Her chatty letters, her subtle humor and because she, too, lived in a city entirely new to her, San Francisco, and shared her own battle with loneliness, we remained good friends. Loneliness comes in waves and, in my case, always became more acute following a visit from American friends.

Warmer weather helped. Flowers bloomed in abundance. I loved walking through the city and there was always a new path to be explored. Cheeks took on a rosy glow and eyes sparkled even under sometime cloudy skies because real warmth is in the people, not the weather. I am once again reminded that back in the 60's every day on the Champs Elysees was, for the Parisians, an Easter Parade. Sundays most of all.

I was definitely in love with this city where people were able to draw on its warmth and in return, lend it warmth. People who seemed to feel what they were seeing. There are so many of us who see only what we feel. An early evening in the park often ended my day and helped the dinner hour pass unnoticed. Then home for another nocturnal trip into fantasy land.

CHAPTER THIRTEEN

Deauville is packed with France's smartly sophisticated, internationally renowned and where the internationally renowned do their shopping. Deauville, where broad, vast beaches and boardwalks separate historic, majestic, five-star hotels from the crowds, the *plage* and the endless rolling waves of the *Manch*. Deauville, the Monte Carlo of Normandy.

Trouville, unlike Deauville, was teeming with overcrowded beaches, the lively clutter of middle-class humanity. The middle-class is not necessarily noisier, there are just more of us. The enthusiasm evidenced by cheering volleyball spectators, laughing children chasing one another, the screeching glee of youth splashing about in the surf and sun bathing sun worshipers expressing impatience with an occasional misguided ball are all things representative of us.

All shore-line buildings in France must, by law, set back a minimum of five hundred feet from the high tide line, allowing twenty-four hour public access to the beach. The shimmering water therefore, becomes a view shared by everyone, a view everyone can walk into.

There's a lot of staring in Deauville, beautiful and beautifully dressed women are admired and viewed as they stroll the boardwalk. Are they mistresses of the very rich? The not so rich? Or are they wives?

Trouville beaches are family beaches.

Phyllis Demarecaux

The real differences between Deauville and Trouville are price and style. People in Deauville dress 'up' which once again left me thankful to former mother-in-law, Andree, and the wardrobe she'd contributed to my status. People in Trouville, which was really my kind of town, dress 'down'.

I was both startled and intrigued by what, at first impression, appeared to be an astonishingly blatant cast system, but soon realized the two beaches, with the exception of their close proximity, were no different from what we have in the United States. Jones Beach on the Atlantic coast, outside New York City, Coney Island and Rockaway are all Trouville beaches. The upper, upper middle-class and wealthy on the Atlantic Coast go to less accessible and more expensive areas: Fire Island, the Hamptons, Cape Cod and Martha's Vineyard.

My first visit to the Normandy coast was memorable and my escort was pleased by the result of our afternoon promenade on the Deauville boardwalk. I'd dressed my toenails in a brilliant red polish and gone barefoot. The color was accented by a pair of red shorts with a matching halter, covered by sheer white voile that was fully open on the sides but secured by a tie at the waist. A gentle breeze nudged at the voile and played peek-a-boo with my legs as we walked, enough to attract the attention of a host of spectators, both men and women.

Our traditional walk over, I was escorted back to the hotel. "We'll be having dinner at nine," my escort told me, "and do the Casino later. Monday nights are not lively casino nights," he informed me apologetically.

Dinner at nine left me with plenty of time to prepare for the glamorous life. The luxury of a bath where I was not accepting a favor, not imposing on someone else's bath privileges, or increasing someone's electric bill. The room was paid for and the bath was mine. "Twas a consummation to be devoutly wished on."

Seconds after dressing, I realized I'd forgotten to bring a change of shoes. There I was in a white linen knit, pearl-buttoned Pauline

The Color of Dusk

Tregere and the only footwear available was a well worn black canvas rope soled espadrille, good only for kicking about on the beach.

While I didn't expect my escort to go tearing his hair out, he might easily have become annoyed with me. My first husband would certainly have been, but on second thought he would never have invited me on such a date. My second husband would have told me to wear the espadrille.

How could I have been such a dunderhead!

My escort, when he arrived, was simply amused. A few dozen telephone calls later, he located a shop keeper who was willing to help a lady in distress, by now ten o'clock on a Monday night.

Our lady savior welcomed us to her shop in lightly accented English. Her charming boutique was a yesteryear motif. We quickly selected a classic brown and white spectator pump. My escort thanked her for exceptional service with an extravagant gratuity.

Next morning I was told that our next stop would be Caen. The WWII American cemetery above Omaha Beach was overwhelming. Row upon row of endless crosses intermixed with Stars of David. So many dead American boys. Reading their names, walking through the hush of time, I was proud to have been a soldier, proud to have worn the American uniform. It took me back to my meeting with General Omar Bradley during the Korean Conflict. It now seemed to me that I hadn't shown him sufficient respect, that none of us had. We credited Eisenhower with so much, leaving the quietly courageous and unassuming General Bradley without the regard he so well deserved. I was grateful for this new feeling I was experiencing, grateful for the pleasure my escort gave me, grateful for his thoughtfulness and for the no-strings attached, friendship he was offering.

Two continental breakfasts later and we were back in Paris exchanging adieus. His business in France concluded, he was returning to his homeland. His fingers caressed my temple and he placed a gentle kiss on my cheek. He thanked me for keeping him company and I thanked him for a memorable long weekend.

Phyllis Demarecaux

There were a substantial number of black-listed, ex-patriots living in Paris. American film director, John Berry, Joe Losey, Jules Dassin and his son, singer Joey Dassin were among them. It was in Paris they found fame, Paris where they were free to pursue careers the McCarthy accusations in America had destroyed.

While I considered myself comparatively apolitical, I was appalled by what had happened to our country. Sinclair Lewis's *It Can't Happen Here* comes to mind because it can happen here. A Republic is a fragile thing. It depends upon people, people exercising their right to vote. Unfortunately when things are at their best, we tend to become complacent. We may not like the 'tone' politics is taking but we can't be bothered to vote. As long as roads are paved, we have a job or our social security checks arrive on time, we pay scant real attention to what is going on and, as we know has happened in other countries, by the time people wake up, it's too late.

CHAPTER FOURTEEN

I finally reached the point where I felt I could dream in French and decided to give it a try. It actually worked, although the night was an endless series of frustrating interruptions when the word I was searching for in my dream was not yet a part of my vocabulary. I pacified myself in the knowledge that it only takes three to four hundred words to speak a language. After that it's merely a question of vocabulary.

Paris is a city where you can always find a place to sit and dream, to think about life, friendships and God. From vistas at *Montmartre* to sitting atop the Arch of Triumph, even atop one of the fifteenth *arrondissement's* new high rises which line the Seine, you can watch its people, its places, its controlled chaos, its cars, trains, metros and bateau.

The only runners in the river park below are the dogs. Their owners stroll behind them, leash in hand, at a leisurely distance, taking in sun and fresh air and, as often as not, exchanging philosophies with fellow citizens.

Somehow, in spite of their freedom, the dogs seem to limit themselves to a disdainful sniff or two, followed by a cautious circling before they trot or bounce away to rejoin their masters. These latter stoop to offer a distracted caress of appreciation. The dog wags its tail in acknowledgement and rushes off for a new encounter.

Leafless in the winter but not lifeless, the trees along this island park spring forth from a rich, green bed of grass. Blue skies, temperatures in the 40's and a sunny summer-like haze over the city can make a winter day glorious. And yet there are blustery

Phyllis Demarecaux

days of wind and rain with giant drops slashing at window walled protection. An every graying sky and neck tucking, coat hugging weather sneaks in to remind you that winter February has YET a way to go.

A seat in a sidewalk cafe is no place to go if you're looking for a still life. Paris is a city in motion. I see a camion, roof laden with bicycles, a shop window display of children's tricycles. Baby buggies. Broken bumpers.

A spot of cement-circled earth boasts a tree in its embrace and breaks the monotony of concrete blocks. A Dachshund on a leash takes care of a need, its attending mistress feigning interest in a traffic light.

There is the passing impatient roar of automation, acceleration, deceleration, exclamation.

Motorbikes, scooters, motorcycles.

A spark, a sputter, a roar.

Laughter? Yes. Smiling? Often. Contemplation, pensiveness? More often. Speculation? Continually. Tears? Only in the young.

Pedestrians streaming. Clicking cleats, clicking talons. The sound of fine crunching sand on a dusty street. Threads of conversation. Glancing inquisition. Knowing supposition.

Warmed, now by the sun
Cooled now by the shade
Man made. God made
People passing people's pathos.

The French countryside is marvelous. Entire communities often hide themselves behind ancient high stone walls. Crumbling and vine covered, they lead you by auto around the villages, rarely into them where the real story lies. Behind those walls you may find enchanted gardens, the rippling murmur of brooks with foot bridges, ancient water wheels, chateaux with real live water-filled moats and drawbridges still in service, You will almost certainly find a high towered church in the town square, its ancient belfry guardian of the countryside, its sisters shepherding sheep, milk cows, goats and/

The Color of Dusk

or children. You'll see puffing priests sporting knapsacks, peddling their bicycles from one parish to another.

Friends Bernard and Suzanne Huffer went to Spain on a two week vacation and left me the key to their country home in Nainville Les Roches.

Nainville, a small village located near Fountainbleau, was about an hour's bus ride from Paris. It's population at the time of my stay seemed to be about thirty adults and a hundred children. Meat could be ordered at the local shop twice a week, salad three times a week and bread every other day. There was a single outdoor telephone in the village and no gasoline station. Residents did own cars but drove to a Shell station in a neighboring village about three kilometers away.

The town mayor mowed his own lawn. What's more he loaned his lawn to an itinerant carnival as a location for their bumper car unit. These units (rides) were centrally located as is the Midway system used in the States. Many small villages are built on a scaled down version of the Paris circular system.

Taking advantage of this, the carnival folk placed their various units throughout the village. In this way the locals were pretty much able to leave their homes, make a complete tour of the carnival and end up back home without having covered the same ground twice. At the same time older people, the physically challenged or simply people who do not have either the inclination or the financial means for the rides, were able to participate in the ambiance of the festivities without leaving their front yards.

It's a wonderful structure, this circular system. It brings life to every section of a village, town, or city. No corner is left out.

The carnival itself, was pretty much as we know them in the States, with one exception. It took them a full week to set up. If I understood correctly they would be staying three days.

My adventures in shopping and understanding the local French caused a bit of hilarity on one occasion. Just as in the States, different areas of the country produce different accents, different expressions.

125

Phyllis Demarecaux

As close to Paris as Nainville is, there was a difference in the way they speak the language. The incident that gave us all a big laugh was my request for a Camembert cheese. My preference had always been the piece that is softer, riper, almost, but not quite, running.

This day the Matron behind the counter, a spirited talkative woman of about fifty with a healthy, happy appearance, was showing me the third box of Camembert. She lifted the lid and I instantly shook my head 'no'. The cheese was visually too hard for my taste. She was becoming dispirited so in an effort to better describe my preference I asked if she did not have one that was *un peu plus in marche*. (one that had walked a little further)

She, as well as the two shoppers hovering behind me broke into hilarious laughter. The symbolism I had made apparently corresponded with a slang term used by the French, *un Camembert qui marche tout seul.*

(A camembert which walks alone) She got it right on her next selection.

It was an enriching experience, my stay in the wooded countryside village of Nainville les Roches, livened by early rising inhabitants and the carnival. I'd toasted myself in the garden, walked, read, slept and dreamed about home, about the Montana Big Sky, the panoramic Yellowstone-Missouri river valley appearing abruptly over the precipice of a rolling plains horizon, about fresh water mountain streams, canoeing on Lake MacDonald, fly fishing outside Lewistown and sunbathing off Whitefish Lake, about Missoula, Philipsburg and yes, even about Sidney. I consumed American style breakfasts of the old West variety, Parisian lunches of salads, cheese and desert and four o'clock teas. Evenings I ate the morning's blessings. (For the uninitiated, blessings are left-over food which received their benediction at a previous meal.)

It was a lazy two week restful reverie. It made me somewhat homesick but it gave me the courage to return to Paris to face one more winter of probable loneliness, but it also told me that I was not alone.

CHAPTER FIFTEEN

My astonishingly expensive electric bill gave testimony to the unrelenting cold winter. I'd just come in from class at the *Alliance Francais* and was making small talk with the Lehman's maid in the hallway in front of her room. She shivered, unlocked the door to her room and swung it open. My cold cramped body cells hummed happily at the unexpected blast of warm air. A glimpse into her room revealed a bright red patch of color coming from the coils of an electric floor heater,.

I made a hasty retreat to my room where a closer look at the electric meter revealed that it was merrily clicking away in spite of the fact that I had absolutely nothing branched into the outlet.

It was probable that my suspicions were well grounded.

Next morning before leaving, I pulled the lever on the counter, effectively shutting down the electric supply. I returned five hours later to find the place in an uproar. The Lehman's maid had no electricity.

Poor thing.

It took about five minutes to heat her room, yet this girl who spent ten to twelve hours away every day, was leaving the heater on for the full twenty four.

Because I paid no rent, it had been agreed that I would pay my own electricity. While I knew that I was paying for the maid's room as well as my own, the cost with my $25 dollar a week income, was leaving me next to nothing for food and school. I explained my

Phyllis Demarecaux

dilemma and we came to an agreement. I could continue paying the electric bill on condition that the maid behave more responsibly in her consumption of electricity. There was even a vague possibility that, with her cooperation, I might end up being able to get a heater for myself.

Other things were looking up as well. Corinne, whose friendship I had learned to greatly appreciate had recommended me as her replacement in the publishing house. She had been hired primarily for her English and that, plus my background experience in publishing, I should be, she told me, a shoe in.

Why was she doing this?

She was off to Kenya to spend time with her father before beginning a special Sorbonne class for future interpreters.

The offices, she told me, would be moving to the Left Bank, *rue des Carmes*. I would be working with an Assistant Director, Jean Gouget, a well-read, bright guy who was about my age. You will like him, Corinne told me. You'll enjoy each other's sense of humor, share each other's sense of irony and he'll be patient about your French.

Her assurance that I would be hired was correct. I began working for ODEJ in September 1962 almost two years to the day of my arrival in Paris.

A letter from my mother November 1962 was encouraging. It sounded as though she'd come to grips with the post Darrel's death period.

Our father, she said, had gone off to Glasgow with another load of furs, beaver and mink. *"He goes more often than he used to. It's coming close to clean up time for the hide pit, too, so I 'spose he'll be loading the truck and going back again soon after his return. It keeps the place peaceful, she said, and the house clean and I stay home more often.*

"I'm also trying again for a birth certificate. With all that's going on in the South, they might become less stringent about Indians, too. Not that it'll make much difference. All the good years are behind me where retirement and social security could have meant something. This way

128

The Color of Dusk

it'll mean didley squat when it comes. If it ever does. Do they pay social security to wives who 'don't exist' when their husbands die?"

She went on to say that she enjoyed the almost daily post cards of Paris which I was sending. She was sharing the wonderful tour with her sister, Florence. "The post man loves them, too," she added. "He asked me if you expect an answer to everyone of them.

"Do you?"

It was the best, well written letter I'd ever received from her. While she was my only faithful correspondent in the family, her letters could usually be filed in the "how are you, we are just fine" slot.

Was she suggesting that someone in the AA group had gotten to her?

Our mother was a strong willed woman. Life had never frightened her….Never until our father, drawing in the guilt of his infidelity and knowing that the best defense is an offense, accused her of being an irresponsible mother, responsible for our brother's death.

The tone of her letter left me feeling she was asking for help, that she was needy. Was she breaking out of the fog that had settled over life since the day she took her first drink? Whatever the cause I decided it would be wise to be prepared should I be needed. Small pox vaccinations were still required to get into the United States so it was important to have mine updated. I took off work at four o'clock that day and made my way to the American Hospital in Neuilly.

"You can't leave Paris," my co-workers were telling me. You've just received your work permit." They continued plummeting me with questions until I simply told them my mother was not well and that I felt I should be prepared. Mom, in those early years, had been the person to whom I could confide anything. She had never punished me for telling a truth, even when the truth revealed misbehavior. She did not judge. She taught me to judge myself merely by inquiring what I thought about what I had done. Her amazing empathy always came through.

129

Phyllis Demarecaux

The hospital in Neuilly was a long way by bus and in less time than it took me to get there I was vaccinated and chasing after a bus back to Paris, a bus with a driver who seemed dedicated to leaving me behind.

Disgruntled, I prepared myself for a fifteen minute trot toward the Paris city limits where, if I didn't get lost in the dark, I would find a *Metro* station. I turned to go back to the sidewalk like a proper pedestrian when I spotted a taxi heading my way.

There I was, a skirt hiked to knee level, head swung back and thumb in the air. The taxi came to a theatrical halt and the passenger, a man wearing a lovely dark cashmere fedora, leaned across the back seat, swung open the door and invited me in. I slid onto the seat next to him, demurely smoothing my skirt down over my knees. It was difficult to make out his features in the gloom of the cab. The hat, handsome as it was, didn't help.

"I just missed the bus," I said.

"No problem. I'm glad to be of help. Where would you like to be dropped off?"

"The *Etoile* will be fine." I told him. We traveled for a few minutes in silence then, "What were you doing at the hospital?"

"My traveling companion picked up some kind of bug in India. And what are you doing in Paris? You're obviously an American."

"I celebrated the end of my second year here in September."

"Doing anything special?"

"Studying French."

"Why don't you tell me more about it over five o'clock tea tomorrow?" he suggested, smiling as the taxi pulled up to the corner of avenue *Kleber.* He handed me his card. "You can reach me at the *Meurice.*"

"Thank you, Mike McEwan," I said, reading his name from the card. "An Irishman. I like that. My father is Irish." I hopped out of the car and gave him a smart salute, a hangover from my days as a WAC. He looked a little surprised, but returned it with gusto.

130

The Color of Dusk

Monique Gelard, myself and the boss, Armand Beressi worked in the office the next day, boxing papers for storage and archives. We had showed up at eleven but didn't get started working until one. The first hour zipped by over lunch and the second because Monique, having purchased a new record player, had brought her old one for me. She hesitated about offering it to me, but I was very pleased. Old for her was new for me.

Five o'clock we closed the final box of archives, our boss added it to the pile we had accumulated and we all sat back to relax.

I told them I could be having tea with a distinguished American gentleman, which lead to an account of my previous evening's adventure. By the time I'd finished, Beressi was on the telephone speaking to yesterday's Mike McEwan. It was his fault he was telling McEwan. He personally would drop me off at the hotel within the hour.

Paris, my new boss explained, is a city where people expect the unexpected and it is part of our job to keep it that way. The Parisians, he said, would never forgive me for spoiling their reputation.

I recognized my American gentleman immediately in spite of his unexpected snow white hair. His hat, youthful countenance and the fact he'd stopped to pick me up, had given me the impression he was younger.

"What kind of boss do you have?" He greeted me with a mild wonder. "Are all Frenchmen like that?"

He was walking me toward the hotel bar and lounge.

"Well, I'm here, but unless my memory is awfully short, the invitation was for tea."

"No problem." We left the hotel and walked up the *Champs Elysees.*

"Your boss woke me from a heavy nap. I wasn't exactly expecting you to show up."

Over coffee I explained my reason for being at the hospital and he told me he was a lawyer, specializing in International Law. It had been a long trip and he and his business partner, who was now out

131

Phyllis Demarecaux

of the hospital, were due back in the States the next day. I learned that he was divorced, lived in Connecticut, had one son about my age and that he hoped one day to make a new life for himself.

I, too, had hopes of creating a new life for myself, but I was doing it in France, I told him. I'd progressed from not speaking the language to speaking fairly fluently. Now it was a question of vocabulary and working on understanding the people and their culture.

We followed coffee with a walk up the *Champs Elysees,* a forgettable movie and finally, dinner on *Fouquet's* sidewalk terrace at the corner of *Avenue Georges V.*

The evening ended with McEwan excusing himself for calling an early finish to our pleasant evening together. His plane back to New York was leaving early the next day. He startled me when he headed for the taxi stand and offered to drop me off at the *Etoile.* I'd forgotten about my little lie. I give him a quick no. Not necessary. The *Etoile* was just around the Arch.

"Thank you, Mike McEwan. It's been an unexpected pleasure."

"For me also," he said, getting into the cab. "Remember, my address is on the card. Stop in and say hello next time you're in New York. I'll buy you another dinner."

"You can count on it," I told him.

He turned in the cab and waved through the back window as it pulled away.

CHAPTER SIXTEEN

Seventeen days before Christmas I was called to the Personnel Director's office. My anxiety level shot into overload. Was I potentially redundant?

Hachette Publishing needed an interpreter for a French journalist who was to interview an American pilot. A VIP I was told. They thought I could handle it.

The VIP turned out to be Jacqueline Cochran, a super woman and pilot who was as legendary as Amelia Earhart. She held the world record for breaking the sound barrier in the Mach II.

Not the women's speed record.

The world's speed record.

According to what I had read Mrs. Cochran's husband, Floyd Odlum, was also a major achiever. At one time known as the fifth richest man in the world, he was one of the original founders of the Atlas Corporation for Public Investments as well as a former executive of the old RKO Motion Picture Studios. My sources, I confess, were movie magazines, not the Wall Street Journal. Ms. Cochran was, however, alone on this trip. She had scheduled exactly thirty minutes of her time for the reporter on condition that the interview take place in her suite at the *Hotel Crillon, Place de la Concorde.*

She wasn't particularly striking, yet something about her contradicted the ordinary. She was a well-groomed natural blonde. Fashionably, if not exceptionally, well dressed. She had a classic,

Phyllis Demarecaux

mid-forties body, somewhat athletic and just this side of stocky. Her hands were wide palmed with short stubby fingers. No smooth streamlined, long nailed gloss here. A hardworking girl's hands. And, as I was soon to learn, she was very proud of them.

Whatever the essence that makes an ordinary looking person stand out in a crowd, Ms. Cochran had it. She was, to me, the kind of person about whom you might ask, but not the type you would ask for an autograph.

The interview began in a very traditional manner, but the one interviewed was anything but traditional. Did she fly over in her own plane? No. Pan Am was delivering some new Constellations to Ethiopia and she went along for the ride. By invitation. Was she driving in Paris? Her reply: "Drive! In Paris! Flying in a torrential storm would be mild in comparison. No" Taxis were serving her purpose.

Ms. Cochran was a real contradiction. Shy on one hand and on the other, surrounded by press photographers, she was a star and enjoying herself.

"You're getting an accent," she told me. "You should come back home. It'll be Christmas soon. If you're willing to leave tomorrow morning and don't mind losing a few days traveling, I can put you up...I mean all the way to our ranch in Indio, California."

"Indio?"

"Indio is in the desert at the south-western tip of California."

The enormity of her offer was slow to sink in.

I remember her walking across the room and resting her arm on the fireplace mantel. "I'd like to help you get home for Christmas," she finished simply.

I spent the night wrestling with my thoughts. My mind was a caldron of emotion, disorientation, indecision, my bedding a knot of twisted discomfort. I was still asking myself if I'd understood Ms. Cochran's offer correctly when, at exactly 10:50 the next morning she opened the door of her hotel suite. She smiled, invited me in and

The Color of Dusk

went back to the telephone where she continued her conversation. I sat down and studied her as she spoke.

"Just bring us back a good story," my boss had said.

She was part of a world that was foreign to me. I'd met rich people on either side of the Atlantic. Rich, but not famous. Most European rich I met led their lives with quiet dignity and without pretension. The former royal residing in castles furnished with century old hand-me-downs, are comfortable and secure in the well-worn clutch of the family history surrounding them. The beauty of their domiciles is dependent upon the period and taste of the Architect. Giant rooms, with the aid of interior decorators, impart warm feelings of welcome into their grandeur. Wealth spells simplicity.

Not always true in the States where the rich and riches are most often younger. Inherited wealth, from first generation success, is often wasted by the pretentious excesses of beneficiaries who attempt to buy their reputations rather than work for them.

Ms. Cochran's world of riches and fame made her more susceptible to whatever extravagances the press might choose to paint of her private life.

Her conversation ended, she turned her attention to me. "Sorry about that. I am an agent for Ricci sales in the States. My attempt is to help women emphasize their own special feminine beauty." The phone rang again. This time it was the French publisher of her autobiography, "The Stars at Noon".

"What kind of illustrating do you call that?" she greeted her caller, referring to her book. "I was a poor kid but I wasn't in rags. You've got me looking unkempt, unwashed! Poor people wash just like real people, damn it. Clean it up!"

Watching her I was reminded of something George Bernard Shaw had said. The world is full of money but real genius or extraordinary accomplishment is very rare.

At noon we shared a light lunch in her suite, disturbed only once by a last minute gift delivery. Two pounds of fresh caviar in a

135

Phyllis Demarecaux

heavy bag filled with ice. "The Editor," she announced, reading the card. "As good a bribe as any, but they still made me look like hell!

"I suppose I should be grateful they're publishing the book. And I am. But the fact that I'm a 'personality' shouldn't give them free license to make me look like a damn beggar. Why do they think it is necessary to exaggerate the difference between my lifestyle then and my lifestyle now? Things were tough enough. What's wrong with truth?"

"Picasso said, 'Art is the lie that tells the truth', Ms. Cochran. Painting words is also an art so maybe that's what it's all about."

"He was right, of course," she responded. "I apologize for *kvetching* - that means complaining, in case you didn't know. My life probably seems idyllic to many people."

The arrival of a courtesy limousine was announced and we departed. Ms. Cochran relaxed, lit a cigarette and breathed in deeply. It was the first time I'd seen her smoke.

"It'll be wonderful getting back to Floyd and the ranch." She closed her eyes and allowed herself to drift into some very dear, private world of her own. It wasn't the first time she'd mentioned her husband. A fair number of years separated them and I suspected his ability to finance her early career had gone a long way toward helping her attain the success she eventually achieved. It seemed unusual to me that she didn't mention him in her book, but Floyd Odlum, I was soon to learn, was not the kind of man who would want 'credit'.

"I suppose Floyd will need a haircut," she continued in this new lady-next-door, manner in which she was acquainting me with yet another facet of her character. "Generally when I get home from a trip, he needs one. What's more," she added with a broad grin. "I'm the barber. A pretty good one too. At least Floyd thinks so". Again she smiled and closed her eyes. "He married me, he said, because I was an all around girl who knew a lot about insignificant necessities and above all, how to handle her boot straps… I like to think he also thought me sexy," she added, laughing.

The Color of Dusk

"So tell me about yourself, Phyllis. And, by the way, please call me Jacqueline. How does it feel to be a beautiful woman in Paris?"

"I'm not sure I know. I mean, my parents never made a fuss over the way we looked, my sisters and I, other than to occasionally tell us that we looked 'nice'. I never heard anyone call me beautiful until I came to Paris and mostly, I have to say, it makes me self-conscious."

"Difficult to understand for someone as ordinary looking as myself."

"You're anything but ordinary, Ms…Jacqueline. You're an attention getter. You've accomplished something extraordinary in your life, something that will one day contribute in some way, either directly or indirectly to the lives of us all. It's created an aura you'll always carry with you."

"Maybe I'm not an ordinary person, but I am ordinary looking. I've always wondered what it would be like to walk into a room and capture attention because of my looks rather than because of who I am."

"Nothing like that has ever happened to me. I'm sure if it had, I would have noticed."

"Not necessarily. Not if you place so little importance on the way you look."

"I guess. if I give it some thought, I know I've met people who were attracted to my face, but it's just the face I grew up with. It's not easy to look in a mirror and equate the image I see with the person other people see and the person we believe we are or who we think we are."

The Limousine pulled to a stop alongside the Departure curb at Orly International Airport. A young PR man appeared instantly and opened the door. "Welcome to Orly International. I've come to help facilitate your departure," he said, and taking the odd pieces of hand luggage, including the caviar on ice, he steered a sure path through the hubbub of general confusion toward the VIP lounge. The redcap who met us, his loaded pushcart and I, followed.

Phyllis Demarecaux

First class boarding was announced seconds later. "We couldn't get you into first class," she apologized.

She turned to wave as she crossed the short strip of field toward the first class entrance. A wintry gust of wind caught the loose ends of her scarf and it, too, waved gaily at the crowd on the overhead observation platform.

Ms. Cochran did wander back to see me during the tourist class dinner service. She dropped into the empty seat beside me. "If you don't mind," she said. "Once we get to New York there won't be much time to get acquainted."

She'd brought with her a plate of first class *hors d'oeuvres* to "ward off hunger," she said, and a couple glasses of champagne which were "certain to leave us thirsting for more."

I don't remember a great deal of our conversation. I did ask her if she made many trips "like this." Her reply: "Not really. The ride to Ethiopia was for fun and PR and I had business in Paris."

With the words of my boss, "bring back a good story." still in mind, I queried her opinion of commercial aviation. Was there any special way that she felt it could be improved?

The passenger in front of her chose this moment to drop his seat into a reclining position. The back-of-the-seat table, which was down, hit Jacqueline in the stomach.

"Put alarm bells on seats and give passengers more knee space," she said, laughing as she attempted to wipe up a small portion of champagne which had slopped onto her table.

Normally, at least in tourist class, the seats aren't supposed to be reclined during dinner hour. I hadn't done much air travel, but enough to know that people need to be taught passenger etiquette.

Jacqueline Cochran was living an exciting life. She'd worked hard to make her dream of flying come true, but, she told me, it was only a fairy tale until Floyd came into her life. Had she been born into this kind of life, it would probably have seemed ordinary, but, she said, she wasn't, and every day of her life was a miracle.

The Color of Dusk

What about your life she was asking me. Any special reason that I chose Paris. Sure there was. Jacques' mother and step father spoke so often, so nostalgically and lovingly of the city that it enthralled me. I wanted to build a new life. Paris seemed an exciting place to begin.

"Without speaking the language?" She sounded skeptical.

"New in every way. Language, culture, traditions."

"Without meaning to sound like a nagging parent, I think ultimately you'll discover your best chances are at home in America. No other country is so oriented toward the freedom of the individual. That alone puts Americans in first place before they even reach the starting line…"

I watched her make her way down the aisle. She stopped several times, speaking to passengers, smiling, especially at the children. Her interest in them, as Vice President of the airline, was understandable but not necessary. Did she have children? She hadn't mentioned any and I assumed she was childless, which perhaps accounted for her attraction to them. Was her case similar to mine? Was Floyd Odlum her first husband?

Information I could find out in research but not the kind of questions I would ask a woman, a celebrity, who arranged my free trip from Paris to the South West Coast of California.

The excitement of all that had happened was mounting, becoming real as we neared the approach to New York City's Idlewild International airport. Having been so awed by Ms. Cochran's astonishing offer, I'd packed my bags and left with exactly nine dollars in my handbag and without a single serious thought as to what would happen when we reached Indio. It could be a problem, but problems, I'd long ago learned, were easily solvable if we maintain our relationship with God. My emergency New York 'get home' bank account would be enough to get me to San Francisco, into Montana and back to Paris.

We were met in the airport by Mr. Cox, who was introduced as Ms. Cochran's General Manager. He led her to a Customs Inspector

Phyllis Demarecaux

who made himself instantly available. I was shown into a line next to her.

Unlike today's world, English was being spoken all around me. It was like participating in a dream that hadn't caught up with reality. Not even my arrival in France had affected me this way. But, of course, I'd had six days on the *Liberte*. Time enough to acclimate not only to the disparate lives and languages about me, but to experience no jet lag.

"Anything to declare?" The no-nonsense clip of his voice brought me back to attention.

"No, Sir."

"What have you been doing in France?"

"Work and school."

"Two years, by your passport. And nothing to declare?"

"The trip wasn't planned."

"You're not a Commie are you? Some black listed actor?"

"I beg your pardon."

"We'll have to open your bag."

"Then do it. I'm not traveling alone and I don't want the others held up because of me."

The man was thorough. My entire bag was undone and it was left to me to repack it. What had he been looking for? He didn't say and I didn't ask.

Once through customs Mr. Cox led me outside to a waiting 1962 Rambler Station Wagon. Ms. Cochran was behind the wheel.

"Give you a hard time, did they?"

"A couple of McCarthy style questions and a bag search. I'm sorry it kept you waiting."

I was attempting to re-acquaint myself with the landscape that was whizzing by. Billboard advertising everywhere. Delicatessens, gas stations, diners, restaurants, produce markets. And huge cars. No wonder small cars weren't popular in the States. Who would dare drive them in this kind of traffic?

The Color of Dusk

Things looked so different, so new. It was like a movie. They'd changed the set. Queens Boulevard was almost unrecognizable. Changes like these didn't happen in Paris, at least in those days. You could count on the city's look to remain pretty much the same no matter how long you were gone. America was a new country, a more progressive place. We build for the future and when the future catches up with us, we build again.

Buildings in Paris were built for the future, too. They were just built with a different kind of future in mind. All of that would, of course, change, and did. High rises along the Seine in the fifteenth arrondissement and breaking up the look of infinity down the *Avenue de la Grande Armee* from the top of the *Arch de Triumph.* Thank you, President Pompidou.

The Manhattan skyline thrust itself onto the horizon. The difference was mind-boggling. While New York City wasn't my birthplace, I'd lived here almost eight years and loved it. The electricity of its collective masses gave witness to the eruption of a sudden flood of emotional turmoil. No matter how often I'd seen it in the past, the thrill of expectation soared.

Riverhouse in Sutton Place was home in New York to the Cochran-Odlum family. A seventeen room apartment overlooking the East River with Roosevelt Island and the Borough of Queens in the background, I gave the view a long hard look, searching for my apartment building in Sunnyside, Queens. I didn't find it and gave up the search with an indifference that surprised me. There was no nostalgia, no curiosity. It was confusing. I was experiencing more nostalgia for the city than for the life I had led as one of its residents. Would it someday be different with Paris?

An inlaid floor pattern in the entrance was an enormous compass.

The needles indicated the directional layout. Showcases along the walls displayed trophies, citations, medals, awards, honorary degrees and ribbons dating from the day she'd received her first license to pilot small aircraft.

141

Phyllis Demarecaux

Ms. Cochran excused herself and went to work. A short tour of the place was enough to see that the luxury of the apartment lay in location and spaciousness. Too much furniture took away whatever special effect some of the individual pieces may have offered and the decorator obviously had a penchant for dark. In general I found the apartment's living areas dreary. The river views and the spacious rooms were in themselves, however awesome.

I retired to my brighter, lighter bedroom to make telephone calls. Several attempts to reach my parents proved frustrating. They were neither at home nor at work. Neither was my former mother-in-law in New York City available. Her daughter, Tatiana Kreinine, however, was. She kept telling me to stop putting-on a French accent. Her comments lent support to Ms. Cochran's jesting when she indicated to me I was losing my American accent.

The following evening, carrying our boots in brown paper bags, we taxied to Radio City Music Hall where Ms. Cochran treated me to the annual Christmas Spectacle. It was beautifully costumed, magical choreographed, orchestrated and colorful.

Our walk back to Riverhouse was exciting. Large fluffy snowflakes cushioned our passage through surprisingly populated streets. The cold seemed gentle, the people benevolent, Christmas friendly, the atmosphere hushed. I realized I missed the snow. We stopped for a moment of prayer in Fifth Avenue's Saint Patrick's Cathedral at Ms. Cochran's request. Next to the centuries old Notre Dame in Paris, Saint Patrick's appeared new. We welcomed the quiet reverence.

Once back on the street we made our way to Riverhouse in companionable, serene silence.

That night my dreams were reassuring. I was in Paris and the language was French.

CHAPTER SEVENTEEN

Next morning found us on our way to New York Marine Airport where Ms. Cochran's twin engine, fourteen-passenger Load Star stood waiting. Our group included Ms. Cochran's maid of twenty-three years. Mr. Odlum's nurse, who had been vacationing in Europe, the co-pilot, to whom I was never officially introduced, Ms. Cochran, myself and Mr. Cox who would be returning to River House.

The flight plan made, the co-pilot in the cockpit, Ms. Cochran at the controls and we were cleared for take-off. I attempted to make conversation on the flight with the women but it was difficult. Their attitude toward me was respectful, but aloof. I was their employer's guest.

Our initial overnight stop was in Washington D.C. My first view of the country's capitol. A solid round of patriotism washed through my veins as Jacqueline dipped a wing and circled the White House.

That evening I was one of Ms. Cochran's ten guests at the Wright Brothers Memorial Award dinner. She, herself, was one of the special guests seated slightly above us on the speaker's platform. There were speeches but I was too awed to pay much attention.

Following dinner I had the pleasure of dancing the twist with Air Force Chief of Staff, Curtis LeMay. LeMay, as I remember him, was a barrel-chested man, slightly overweight but light on his feet and an excellent dancer. He danced me breathless and I enjoyed myself immensely.

Phyllis Demarecaux

Next day we flew to Atlantic City, Missouri and the third day to Amarillo, Texas. Leaving Amarillo, Ms. Cochran adjusted the flight plan to include the Grand Canyon because she had overheard me tell the co-pilot I'd never been there. The United States of America were indeed spectacular, individually and awesome in their entirety.

Heating meals on the plane was fascinating. Because things boil so quickly at high altitudes, we were forced to bring them to a boil repeatedly before they actually became hot. It was one of those little facts we learn in school but until actually confronted with the problem, it doesn't mean much.

Repeated efforts to contact my family at each of our stops continued to be fruitless. Sharon and her husband were living in Williston, North Dakota. A nurse, she was probably working in one of the local hospitals. I had no idea where Jane was working but felt certain she and her husband were back in Sidney, having recently moved from Plentywood. It would be easier to use the phone in my friend Claudia's new home in San Francisco. Reaching her was a welcome relief. She accepted my collect call and would be expecting to hear from me as soon as I knew exactly when I'd be arriving.

Indio, California was exciting. Seeing the desert in full bloom was a glorious sight. The cotton buds were bursting open, their whiteness glittering in the sun and the date harvest was beginning. Tangerines, grapefruits and green, green foliage everywhere unexpectedly turning the desert into a visual paradise. To the left, upon entering the driveway leading toward the main house, orchid trees, soon-to-be in full bloom. To the right, a rolling green, mesquite-treed, nine-hole golf course. Mr. Odlum, I was told, frequently opened the course to the public.

Giant Mesquite trees had been trimmed of underbrush, tamed and domesticated. The weird contorted pattern of their vine-like trunks, their feather-like, transparent green leaves of fluff, generated the feeling of a Japanese silkscreen print.

144

The Color of Dusk

The living and principal room of the main house measured a gigantic sixty by seventy-five feet. Almost as long as the high school gym in my home town, Sidney, Montana.

"Approximately," Ms. Cochran appended. The room was built around a Rumanian carpet. It had been woven in a single piece and was to be displayed at the 1939 World's Fair. With war waging in Europe and the cancellation of the Fair, the carpet was put up for sale.

This home she had made with Floyd Odlum was completely in touch with nature. Extensive use of all the natural elements of the desert in the landscaping had been superbly handled.

A giant stone-block fireplace, the size of my maid's room dominated the far end of that giant living room. It's backdrop, also of stone, was an Inca Indian woman in native dress, the soft luminous colors were ground into the very stone from which she was carved. Inside the fireplace at either end, small two-seater benches welcomed seriously adventurous toe warmers. A wood carving of Christ dating back to Cortez decorated the mantelpiece.

Floyd Odlum's simple "Good morning" left me feeling he'd given me something good, intangible, but precious. He spoke briefly to his wife and withdrew with a nod in my direction. I was told he suffered from severe arthritis and did little socializing. He did, however, the second day after my arrival, send his nurse to ask if I might join him at the pool that afternoon while he did his exercises. I felt extremely honored. He quizzed me endlessly about my life in France. I spoke of my romance with the French language and with Paris.

"And yet," he remarked somewhat quizzically, "you spend your time there housed in a maid's room."

"Yes," I remember telling him, he was right, but once outside I walked into the same city as did its richest and its poorest inhabitants.

I commented on his collection of rocks and, because he was missing a Montana agate, I promised to send him one. The agate I sent was beautifully polished by my father. However, it never arrived. Apparently there was an error in the address I had noted and it was

145

Phyllis Demarecaux

returned. I felt very badly about it because the rock collection was the only thing I'd seen in the house that was totally personal to Floyd Odlum.

I questioned him about his life, as well. His reply was something on the order of: "I am an old man who suffers from arthritis and who has just spent time with a beautiful young lady who has given me the pleasure of her company."

As he spoke his nurse approached with a large bath towel. A look of immense compassion swept across her face as she watched him, excruciatingly pained, pull himself from the water and wrap the towel around his body. She led him to a motorized wheel chair and we bid good-bye with a wave on my part, a nod of the head on his.

Money from my meager New York bank account arrived a couple of short days later and I did not see him again before leaving.

As special as it was, my visit in Indio left me feeling nostalgic for the ordinariness of my Paris home. A place where I felt more like a person. Here, in Indio, with these extraordinary people in this extraordinary setting, it was as though I had been brought to marvel, to be awed and to be humbled. Ms. Cochran told me that she, herself, had never gotten used to it. Perhaps she too, wasn't certain she belonged.

We all, in some way, feel we're living a lie because the person we know as ourselves can never completely be the person seen by others.

As a good-bye visit to my room in the guesthouse proved, Jacqueline Cochran had not finished astonishing me.

"Floyd likes you very much," she told me, "and thought perhaps you might be more interested in coming back to the States knowing you have a job. We need another helping hand here to help keep our lives in order. Help things run smoothly.

"If you want to know more about what the job entails, talk to Ruth. She's in the front office of the building on your right as you enter the property. Take her number. Give her a call if there isn't time to see her before you leave."

Her kindness left me speechless. "Think it over," she said. Yes, I did. Over and over and over.

CHAPTER EIGHTEEN

The Greyhound Bus trip up the rugged California coast was worth every astonishingly scenic moment. Somehow the grandeur of the Pacific was beyond that of the Atlantic, the vastness of it beyond the widest of the wide-angle lenses, its color deeper, its blues bluer. The shudder of its waves was like a massive, unrelenting series of unbeatable enemies as they charged, retreated, regrouped and attacked. Again and again and again. In spite of its potentially powerful invincibility it presented a gentler facade, tamer to my eyes, infinitely more awesome.

The anticipation of seeing my friend Claudia, as well as the family, kept me company as the bus rolled on. Separate destinations, but destinations, as Ms. Cochran had said, are, like destiny, in constant fluctuation. Life, when the gift is lived is always in transit. Would I tell them about the offer? I thought not. Pressure from the outside could mean the final decision wouldn't necessarily be my own.

My visit with Claudia was limited to two days. Her dream was to introduce me to her beloved San Francisco, just as mine would have been to introduce her to Paris. But she understood that I wanted to be with my family for Christmas so we spent our first day talking, catching up on the emotions of life which are so difficult to express in writing. Our fears. Our hopes. Our phobias. Our faith.

The evening was spent at a party given by Claudia's French class. An ideal occasion, she suggested, for showing off my French. Her

147

Phyllis Demarecaux

class, she said, was limited to reading. Why would they choose to make themselves appear inadequate by talking when reading and writing could get them straight A's?

She was actually hoping that I would flush out the truth by speaking French to a couple in the class who had said that they already spoke French. None of the class had ever heard them in conversation. Not even between themselves. Had Claudia told me this before the party, I would have definitely challenged them!

"Think of it this way," I said, quoting Theo Schuker, a friend of mine.

"We all have a working knowledge of at least four languages. The one we speak; the one we read; the one we write and the one to which we listen."

There was a wonderful African-American at the party. A kind of James Baldwin, destined to become the love of Claudia's life. They spent the entire evening and into the wee hours talking literature and ideas.

As a result we arrived home exhausted, overrode the alarm and woke too late for the outing. "The only air conditioned city in the United States", Claudia bemoaned, "and you've seen so little of it."

Ah but we always found so much to talk about. Claudia, after her discharge, was the only person I knew who had to compete with her grandmother for top marks when getting her degree. It was difficult because Claudia had to work her way through while her grandmother didn't have to surmount that obstacle. She had all her time to study. Nevertheless, Claudia won, but, she said, "barely".

It was a thrill hearing about her adventures and misadventures, her high aspirations for the future, her goals and her plans for realizing them, to see that she'd combated the demons of depression that haunted her and that she had won the battle. We regretted separating, but embraced warmly, vowing to exchange more letters.

My parting words of wisdom to her were, "Never apologize for being brilliant."

The Color of Dusk

My parents, whom I'd finally contacted, had been on a trip through the Black Hills. Mom in particular was happy to hear I was coming home. To our great disappointment my brother Michael, now in the Air Force, hadn't been able to get Christmas leave. My younger sister, Sharon, wasn't with us either. She and her husband were sharing the holiday with his family.

Mom and Dad went for a few drinks Christmas day and forgot to come home, but with that one exception, they remained sober, either in deference to the holiday or to my visit. Jane and I spent time together catching up on one another's life. She was not happy in her marriage but did not delve on the details. She would, she said, once she'd figured things out.

Outside my parents and sisters, I realized I had no close friends. Friends visit each other. Friends bring friends home. Jane, Sharon, and I hadn't wanted to run the risk. We didn't want to be embarrassed by drunken parental arguments. We didn't think we had a 'Home Sweet Home'. Like many kids in small towns, we felt we were most often judged by our parents behavior. Without much more to look forward to, I said good-bye to my parents. It wasn't a decisive good-bye. Whatever decision I was going to make, I had to return to Paris to pick up my things. To do a proper good-bye required a "Thank you" to all the people who had helped me. I couldn't just disappear.

Jane drove us over to Sharon's place in Williston, North Dakota where the three of us spent a great day reminiscing. While Jane made her way back to Sidney, Sharon and her husband, Charles, drove me to Minot where I caught a plane back to New York.

Rather than attempt to get in touch with the former family or friends in the city, I contacted lawyer, Mike McEwen. He said it was an unexpected pleasure to hear from me and made arrangements to be free for an early dinner. We shared a happy evening. I told him about my extra-ordinary trip home and he spoke about the completion of the international deal he had been setting up with Nabisco when I met him. We agreed it would be fun to keep in touch and then, once more, I was on my own.

149

Living alone wasn't something that bothered me. Living in France made me realize that I am, by nature, something of a loner. Living in cold water flats, however, heatless and with endless flights of stairs to climb, was not a future to look forward to. If I stayed, things had to change. On the U.S. side, Ms. Cochran's offer was not to be taken lightly. The contrast in lifestyle made the choice a difficult one. She would need an answer by the end of January.

New Year's day found me on the Air France Super Constellation, flight 011 to Paris. The impact of the forward thrust pressed lightly into my diaphragm pushing my body with agreeable firmness against the high-backed seat. We were airborne.

It's a different time, I was telling myself. I speak the language. I won't be caught in so many 'situations'. I can tell a joke, go to plays and French movies without having to sit through them a dozen times to grasp their meaning. I can watch television, listen to the news, read newspapers and enjoy magazines. Of course, I could do all those things in the States, too. And probably better.

The first trip had been an adventure. This trip was a reality. When the unfamiliar became familiar would Paris still hold its attraction for me?

"No smoking please. Fasten your seat belts. Transit passengers are requested to wait in the lower lounge. Passengers for Paris follow the green lights…"

I made my way to the baggage claim and hustled up a luggage carrier. They weren't as readily available as in the States, but accustomed to French chaos, I was prepared in a way I had never been before. Customs was efficiently handled and soon I was making my way through the bustling crowd, the baggage handlers, the joyous shouts of welcome and felt the flush of pleasure, the sense of fulfillment.

Leave Paris for a piece of someone else's luxury in a desert where green grass was a paint job renewed annually?

The Color of Dusk

What was I thinking" Where was my head?

As Gertrud Legendre said: ...... "Time to stop contemplating life...Time to live it."

Of course I would stay in France. Paris was my home!

CHAPTER NINETEEN

Tasks required of me were varied upon my return. I typed a number of manuscripts, short stories for children's books which were the publishing house's primary goal. The French keyboard was, of course, different from that of the U.S. I overcame a part of that problem by having the necessary accents placed on those duplicate keys on the keyboard of my own Royal Standard typewriter.

Another task given to me on one particular day was to identify the font used in one of the books we were planning to reprint. Because almost all the books they published were in public domain, their policy apparently didn't require keeping a record of the various details involved in their publications. I was given a stack of one or two hundred single pages, each of a different font. Using the book in question as my guide, it was my job to find the matching font. A seriously tedious process.

About an hour into the job Monique Gelard, the lady who ran that department, looked up and asked me how I was doing.

My response, tone ironic, "Well, it certainly isn't in italics."

She took my silly little joke seriously and began patiently explaining italics and their use. That she would think I didn't know the difference left me speechless and indicated that my future in French publishing might be short lived.

The next of those most interesting assignments with which I was entrusted in my new job included a trip to London. Things were

The Color of Dusk

looking up. I would be meeting with Paul Hamlyn, president and owner of Paul Hamlyn Limited Publishers.

Although tempted upon arrival to do a little sight seeing, I conscientiously made telephone contact with Mr. Hamlyn's secretary. My meeting with him had been rescheduled for the following morning. However, she said, Mr. Hamlyn would be honored to escort me to a casual, get acquainted dinner that evening. I, of course, would be honored to accept his invitation.

The new schedule left me with time to spend with my brother, Michael, who was stationed at the Benwarters/Woodbridge U.S. Air Force base in Ipswitch. Mike was able to get a pass into London and we had a brief, but happy, lunch time reunion.

Following lunch, I decided to get myself dolled up for the big, anticipated evening with Mr. Hamlyn. My first move was to a hairdresser. Back at the hotel, a short nap was the order of the day, followed by a bath in a regally splendid bathtub which must have been at least seven feet long.

I stepped up into the bathroom, adjusted the water temperature, let the tub run full, then slipped out of my robe and with a shiver of pampered anticipation, stepped up to the backend of the tub and let myself slide blissfully into its enticing welcome.

Having totally miscalculated the tub's depth, which was on a level with the lower floor of the bedroom, (at least a foot deeper than expected) I was down under and sputtering bubbles within seconds, my smart new hair-do gone in a splash.

Laughter conquered my indignation.

The damage done, I calmed down and had a delicious, relaxing bath.

I did enjoy Paul Hamlyn's company and we certainly had a good meal but it was the tub and bath that left the most notable impression of that first visit to London.

Back in Paris friend Corinne wanted me to make a foursome out of a dinner date with a gentleman who she felt could eventually become important to her work as an interpreter. The man's name

Phyllis Demarecaux

was Heibert Golsong. (probably misspelled) His exact working title escapes me but he was I believe, head honcho of the Human Rights division of the Council of Europe in Strasbourg, France.

Corinne, along with friend, Pierre de Soultrait and Mr. Golsong, picked me up at my apartment in Paris and we were off to another dining experience.

Corinne and I were seated facing the two men. She in front of Pierre and myself in front of Mr. Golsong. He was an amiable man, married, he said, with children. His way perhaps, of letting me know he was "not available".

The four of us exchanged stories and Corinne, toward the end of the meal, asked how my trip to London had gone. I, of course, began telling them about my introduction to the bathtub luxury. When I came to the slide into the tub, I raised my hand in a demonstrative glide down and across the table. The swoop was broader than intended and my forefingers connected with the stem of Mr. Golsong's glass. Top heavy with wine it tipped and emptied its contents, effectively baptizing him from neck to waist. In the nanosecond it took him to react, I brought my arm back and concluded with a saintly, "In the name of the Father, the Son and the Holy Ghost. Amen." From there, I broke into unrestrained, semi-hysterical laughter.

The others, as well as my victim and the diners seated at tables on either side of us, were all gleefully chorusing the nature of my recovery. Once things calmed down, I was able to offer an apology and was thankful to learn that white wine would not stain. His suit, necktie and shirt would not be ruined. Why did I come up with the Catholic benediction? Probably because to my errant way of thinking most people in France were Catholic.

It had been a chilly evening and Mr. Golsong in his wet suit and no coat, was shivering before we reached the parked car. His parting words when we dropped him off at his hotel were, "It's been a pleasure meeting you. You've made the evening memorable."

We were actually destined to become good telephone friends.

CHAPTER TWENTY

Time to move. The new temporary living quarters were conveniently located next door to my work. The offices, once on the Right Bank, were now in the Latin Quarter's fifth arrondissement on the *rue des Carmes*. I was delighted.

My landlady, naturalized French of Ukrainian origin, was a particularly outstanding woman of about sixty. Her approximate size when seen from the front, was that of a circus fat lady, but not so well proportioned. Seen from the back, her body, was readily recognizable and although enormous, quite shapely. Her breasts, resembling two semi-deflated beach balls, hung down somewhere around her hip line and swung free when she walked. When she sat it was her habit to hoist them up onto her lap where they resided until further movement.

She had a long, very thin gray beard and a fairly heavy mustache that hung over her upper lip. All teeth between the upper incisors were missing.

She smiled often.

She smoked black tobacco, French cigarettes in a holder, and puffed away as much as a third of a cigarette on a single drag. While so doing, her eyes took on a vague, watery withdrawn glaze.

It appeared that her hair had not seen a shampoo for many months.

Phyllis Demarecaux

Worn shoulder length and parted in the middle, it was slicked down in the male fashion of a 1930 Corsican zoot-suiter. She had a voice like thunder quite possibly because of a hearing problem.

Her elbows were endowed with enormous crusts of calloused skin. She spent hours with them propped upon the table in front of her while reading. Finally, she was one of the best read, up-to-date current events persons I've ever met. She suffered from a cardiac condition and hadn't left her apartment for seven years.

I spent about fifteen minutes a day conversing with her and would have spent more, but talking, for her, represented a strong physical exertion. What she did say was always worth listening to.

Photographs of her at age forty reveal she had been fantastically distinguished looking with the classic elegance of a woman of means. The thing that remained remarkably young in her visage was the bright, luminous blue of her eyes. Ukraine blue, I called it, like Vincent Kreinine's, Jacques de Marecaux's step father, my former father-in-law.

The single room I rented was far superior to the earlier maid's room, at least four times larger, furnished with bookcases filled with fantastic collections; buffets darkened with age; four upholstered chairs of an unrecognizable period; two enormous leather arm chairs and a tri-cushioned leather *canapé* rivaling the leather chairs for comfort. The center of the room boasted a table desk that quickly became the center of my life.

One modern beige sofa bed with royal blue cushions sat pushed against the far wall. It obviously didn't fit the *decor* but the room was so packed with furniture its presence simply went unnoticed.

The entire street, *rue des Carmes,* was interesting but the view from my second floor window was the best possible. Directly across the street, set back about twenty feet from the sidewalk and planted between much taller buildings on either side, was a thirteenth century church, *L'Eglise des Carmes.* It's lower height allowed the sun to shine into my room. The street, originally called *Bruneau* according to my history book on the streets of Paris, came into

The Color of Dusk

existence around 1250. It was re-christened *Carmes* round 1317 after the *Carmelite* convent and widened in 1923. The original width was little more than that of a cobblestone footpath. Several buildings lining the original footpath were lost as a result of widening the street for automobiles.

The *Eglise,* I as told, opened occasionally and I looked forward to the day I might visit the interior. My window allowed a glimpse of the *Notre Dame* Cathedral, located on the *Ile de la Cite,* and to my right, the *Pantheon,* a national monument and burial place of France's illustrious. Among those buried there are Francois Voltaire, Victor Hugo, Emile Zola, Louis Braille, Jean Jaures - a left wing politician and orator assassinated in 1914, and second World War resistance leader, Jean Moulin - tortured to death during the Nazi Occupation. Both the *Pantheon* and *Notre Dame* are lit up at night.

All monuments in Paris of any stature are lit until eleven p.m. every night of the week. The city's light work is consistently genial and has earned Paris the world's title as "The City of Light". An evening dinner trip up the Seine on a *Bateau Mouche,* or any one of a number of tour boats, is an enchanting revelation of the city's inspired architecture.

A five minute walk brings me to the Sorbonne University and *boulevard Saint Michel. Place Saint Germain des Pres,* home of the oldest church in Paris (AD 542) and the artists *cafe Deux Magots,* an indoor/outdoor *cafe* where notable people gather to see and be seen. (Jacques Cousteau, Yves Montand, Edith Piaf, Jean Paul Sartre, Francoise Sagon) Famous before the war, the *Deux Magots* was rediscovered, along with Existentialism, after the World War II occupation.

Existentialism was the intellectual rage in Paris after the war, but I discovered most people, myself included, didn't have a clue what it meant. Curiosity and my Webster's Collegiate defined it as a philosophy centered on the analysis of existence and the way we find ourselves existing in the world, while stressing the freedom and responsibility of the individual.

Phyllis Demarecaux

Tourist seeking to glimpse the luminous and famous can always be found at the *Deux Magots*. A single cup of coffee buys seating space for two to three hours. The *Deux Magots,* along with its neighbor, the *Cafe Flore,* supply the most sidewalk seating in the *Place St. Germain.* Across the boulevard *Lipp* is a popular, more serious eatery. It was here that I, literally, ran into Yves Montand vying for the same available table, He won, of course. I was to meet him officially, through friend, Noel Howard, several years later. He actually recalled the incident.

I've forgotten to mention Madame Affinasief's (phonetical spelling) other renters with whom I was sharing the kitchen and bathroom. Married for eighteen months, they still appeared to be blissfully happy. The bride, just sixteen years old, was from Portugal. Her husband, a Frenchman, was twenty-five. She delighted in waiting on and attending to his needs. Her daylight hours were devoted to the laundry, done by hand after heating the water in the kitchen, ironing his twice a day shirt changes, shopping and preparing his meals. Her devotion was limitless; her youthful stamina intact. On those rare occasions when she appeared exhausted she still greeted her husband's evening arrival with a brilliant, adoring smile.

My job became more interesting and pleasurable every day. The people in the editorial division were all talented, intelligent, patient and helpful. Odette Nahaum was our sultry Egyptian office dancer. Monique Gelard, a quiet brunette beauty with the most seniority, was our competent leader. Francine Jabet, our regal beauty, sat in the back of the large, shared office. Her more mature presence reminded us of our duty when the story telling got out of hand. Michelle Lebreton, a gracefully slender cherry blonde with a healthy outdoor beauty, more restrained, but much appreciated, was our visual artist. She handled paste-ups, illustrations, and page make-up. Elizabeth Soutou was our singer. She hummed happily as she worked, a quality we appreciated. Michelle Cohen, a tall willowy beauty with long golden blonde hair and a militant stride, held the illustrious position

158

The Color of Dusk

of Secretary to the President Director General of the company, Armand Beressi.

While Michelle, Monique and Elizabeth became good friends, it was years before we invited each other into our homes. Jean Goujet was more involved with sales than the creative division and as a director was more remote. Surprisingly, he was the first to invite me into his home for dinner.

As time went on I became more involved with the editorial department. Monique discovered I had worked for publishers in the United States. No one had ever asked and I had not volunteered the information during my interview. She began 'borrowing' me to help with the mounting of texts and the typing of manuscripts. I was, she told me, the best and most accurate typists in the office. French students, I learned were not taught the basic skills in public schools. This explained why Francine Jabet, secretary to the assistant director, had a secretary of her own, a secretary who had gone to a trade school and who knew how to type.

Yes, the French *Baccalaureate* is equal to two college years in the States. Although French students receive it without the American requisite of some basic skills, their superior education earns them a comfortable starting salary.

ODEJ was a subsidiary to Hachette, one of, it not *the*, largest publishing house in France. ODEJ published primarily children's books but was destined to branch out beyond *TOUT L'UNIVERS,* the young people's encyclopedia. We became *ODEGE.*

The more adult and equally successful publications were *LES GRANDS PEINTRES* (painters), *LES GRANDS MUSEES* (museums) and *LES GRANDS MUSICIENS,* a five color magazine which included an LP (for the younger generations: a long playing record) of the classical composer of the week.

I enjoyed being one of the company's early employees. I was settling in and loving it.

It was while living on the *rue des Carmes* that I met Corinne's friend, the Count Francois du Bois de Riocour for a second time. We

Phyllis Demarecaux

were in the apartment where she lived with her parents. Francois was on his way out when I arrived and Corinne was asking him to drop a package off with a friend of hers, on his way home. He suggested we have dinner together.

Corinne, he told me in a rye tone, was busy with a journalist friend. I accepted, with Corinne's blessings. He would pick me up at seven. We visited briefly before he left to drop off the package at Christiane Wagner's home. Christiane lived with her three year old daughter in a house that edged its way into the *Parc de Monceau* on the *boulevard de Courcelles,* a long way from my maid's room but in reality only a ten minute walk from *rue Theodule Ribot.*

I dated Francois perhaps a half dozen times. On our second or third date he suggested that my interest in him, assuming there was an interest, was purely platonic. He went on, however, to set up another dinner date, saying my enjoyable company and my healthy appetite would have to suffice. The day set for the following dinner I actually received a telegram announcing that he would be picking me up a half hour later than was originally agreed upon.

He continued dating Corinne and, by now, was also dating Christiane Wagner. Through him I met, among others, the Austrian, S.A.S. Prince Armand Eli Louie d'Arenberg. Armand was a gentle, quiet, ageless, man. Tall and very slender. There was an aroma of sadness about him leaving an impression of loneliness although he was certainly not friendless. I assumed he was married but never saw or heard of a wife the few times we visited. Neither did he speak of children. I didn't ask because he never asked, never a personal question about my background.

Francois was still the consummate diner. The most astonishing invitation I had from him was to spend a weekend at his friend, Armand's chateau. Because he, Francois, would be coming from Germany I was to show up at the Prince's home in Paris, where the two of us would travel together to the *Chateau de Minitou Salon.* I assumed Francois's friend was Christiane Wagner because her mother was still living in Germany where Christiane was born and

The Color of Dusk

I knew that she and he were still dating. Christiane would, in fact, eventually become his wife, the Countess du Bois de Riocour.

The Prince Armand and I took the train. First class.

Lunchtime, to my utter astonishment, he produced a large picnic basket loaded with a salad, a selection of fruits, fried chicken drumsticks and bottles of both drinking water and a red Bordeaux wine. There was a fork suppled for the salad and a paring knife for pealing and slicing the fruit. The Prince, and so I, picked up the chicken in our hands and ate with gusto.

A black Citroen appeared mysteriously at the train station and we were driven to the Chateau. Once we pulled off the main road we wound our way through a small forest of giant trees. The Chateau played peek-a-boo through their leaves as we made our way toward it. What appeared to be the entire staff was standing under a protective cover at the entrance to the building. Our driver pulled the car up in front of them and stopped.

"Bonjour, Monsieur le Prince," they greeted Armand as he stepped from the car. *"Le Prince a fait un bon voyage?"*

I also was greeted with a smile. Armand introduced me to them one by one. They shook my hand and almost bowed as they wished me welcome.

Inside, Armand had me shown to my room where, he hoped I would be comfortable. The Shaw of Iran's former, barren, wife, the Princess Soyora had very much enjoyed her say in this same room, I was told. Francois and His friend would be arriving within a couple of hours.

Cocktails and dinner would be served at 7 pm.

He wished me a good rest.

Dinner was served in an enormous dining room by a single butler who prepared our plates individually and brought them one by one to the table, his crepe soled shoes squeaking every step of the way across the highly polished wooden floor, to and from the buffet. I was seated to the Prince's left. Francois, seated across from me, had arrived and to my astonishment, with a semi-stocky blonde, who

161

Phyllis Demarecaux

spoke English with a subtle accent. What happened to Christiane? Her name was not mentioned. We spent the entire evening speaking English. I have no idea if she spoke French.

It was without fanfare that Francois and His German friend left early the next day. I remained and would be traveling back to Paris the next day, it seemed, with the Prince.

A middle-aged couple showed up for lunch after which the four of us did a tour of the Chateau property. The conversation was lead by the woman who seemed to be deeply informed about the what, when, where, why and how of all that went on in the lives of several dozens of their common acquaintances. The Prince mumbled an occasional "umm" to indicate that he was still there as she continued her report. Her husband corrected a few rare details which his wife had erred upon. I was completely out of it and simply listened. By mid-afternoon the air around us was beginning to vibrate with her curiosity about me but she was too worldly and probably not a close enough friend of the Prince to ask the question directly.

Our tour complete, they bid their adieus. "Who is she?" was left hanging in the air. Armond had deftly skirted all her attempts to find out. I assured him that he could have said I was just nobody, but he said she would have interpreted such a reply as, 'None of your business,' which would have been rude but, he added, "It was none of her business."

We had an informal dinner in a small area, about twice the size of my early maid's room. Flames danced invitingly in the fireplace. Armand shared some photo memory albums with me and at one point, he looked up and quietly asked, "What did you think of my visitors?"

My response was something like this. "Her apparent ability to keep up with so many friends and all that is going on in their lives has to be admirable. I'm just not able to do that kind of thing."

"Yes," he said, his smile as discreet as his question. "Thank God."

CHAPTER TWENTY-ONE

Just shortly after the assassination of President John F. Kennedy, I was given notice, not from ODEGE but from Madame Affinasief, that I was going to have to move. The offices where I worked were being expanded as had been anticipated. She wasn't to be blamed. It would mean a higher rental income for her.

My new home was in the twentieth arrondissement near the *Porte de Vincennes*. It was a "studio" apartment on the first floor facing the court yard with a step-in kitchen and a small, but never-the-less, walk-in closet. The rectangular main room was not much longer than the maid's room where I had initially hibernated but was at least three feet deeper. The rent was minimal.

One entire wall in the tiny kitchen area was taken up by an enormous electric meter which was dripping oil. I contacted the powers that be. Could it be updated? The fellow they sent said that in all his thirty-five years with the company, he had never seen anything like it. Well, neither had I.

Moving was a lighter task than expected. Ex-husband, Jacques de Marecaux, was in town doing a television shoot and volunteered to be the "muscles". The evening of the Wrap party, he invited me to dinner with the crew with which he was working. (Wrap: the closure of the filming)

It was a pleasant evening. He suggested keeping me company his final night in Paris and laughed pleasantly when I replied, "Them days is gone forever." He was married now and I think that his son,

Christian, had already been born although my memory may be faulty. We hadn't done much real visiting. The work of moving was a full time job. He was busy working during the week. So was I. And the only other time we saw each other was at the Wrap party.

The extra wide door to the entrance of my new home was an eyesore. With the written and signed permission from the owner of the studio, I was allowed to make the changes I requested.

My first solution was to install a curtain on the living room wall which ran from the door to the farthest end of the studio, thus serving to hide the entrance to the kitchen as well. I had mahogany cupboards built in along the kitchen wall facing the living room and to the left wall where the new much smaller, electric meter was incorporated. A work table below the cupboards folded against the wall when not in use. The kitchen sink was below the window at the end of the room and the wall to the immediate right, now free of that monstrous meter, left enough space to create a shower. So I did.

A single extra long twin bed served as the sofa. I purchased pillows for the back and sewed up an "upholstered" cover which disguised the original use for which the bed was intended. The closet was a walk-in and to the unfamiliar, appeared to be an additional room.

There was no coffee table.

An ironing board of deluxe dimensions served as a dining table. It boasted a selection of heights and a wire extension which I used for the single hot dish. When not in use it stood hidden behind the curtained wall.

The location of the studio was not ideal insofar as the office where I worked. However it turned out to be a perfect location when my son was born. There was a pilot *Creche* within a block.

Three months into the pregnancy I was taking the required annual physical checkup. Things were not going well. I was immediately taken off work and put to bed. It was suggested that I not stay alone. Alone with no telephone was not an option.

The Color of Dusk

First there was a friend, off on a two month's shoot, who loaned me her studio. I was alone, but there was a telephone. Following her return I went to Corinne de Longevialle's parent's very ample apartment where they housed me in their son Hughes's bedroom. What they were doing to help me was an extraordinary move on their part. Even with their disapproval they accepted me into their home without prejudice, without judgment. I was their daughter's friend.

Because my 'unmarried' condition did not meet with their approval, my stay became a sort of quarantine. I was confined to the bedroom. Meals were brought in on a tray. They were, from their point of view, protecting me from public disgrace or from being put to shame. (Isaiah 54:4-5)

Soft laughter and the hum of conversation filtered down the hall into the room from the frequent small dinner parties they had. Even though some of those parties included friends or acquaintances my presence in the apartment was not revealed. Corinne's father, Guy, had an extensive library which, because I was and still am, an avid reader, filled my days with wonder. Her mother's daily visits were on some occasions as long as two hours. This all ended upon Hughes return.

The months went quietly by. I lost contact with the people at work. No news from Christiane and surprisingly, although her parents housed me, little or no contact with Corinne. Actually she was very busily studying at the Sorbonne's course for future would be interpreters.

It was Guy de Longevialle who told me that my baby would have to be officially recognized, either by myself or the father. It was the law. Should the issue arise, and Sean's father were to discover he was the father and wanted to recognize the child, he would almost certainly be given priority. French law would favor the father. (ie: Working married women, in those days were required to have written permission from their husband before receiving their salary directly. The same for a bank account.)

Phyllis Demarecaux

I went post haste to the *Marie* (court house) and took care of my baby's recognition.

My last stay was with new friend and neighbor, Sylvie Arrayet. Sylvie lived in a new apartment building next door to the building where I was housed. In fact, it was she, who had lived in the studio where I was now housed. Her new residence, although without a telephone, was not a studio, but a comfortable, good sized one-bedroom, bathroom apartment. The idea behind this move was in part because it was close to my own home, but primarily because Sylvie was home most evenings, which, with the exception of her work hours, meant that I was not alone.

It was during my stay with her that my last letter to Claudia was returned. A large black stamp across her address read DECEASED. A brief cold note from her mother followed a couple of days later simply saying that Claudia had committed suicide by swallowing pills. I was stunned.

The grief was intense, so much so, that I began finding it difficult to swallow, difficult to digest. The result was that I practically lived on water the seventh and eighth month of the pregnancy.

The only meal I recall keeping down, although not in its entirety, was when friend, Art Whitman was on temporary assignment in Paris. Art had been my boss on a job briefly held before my divorce from Jacques. It was a pleasure to see him, to have news of common friends in New York and an update on his writing career but I was certainly not my usual energetic self and still depressed over Claudia's suicide. His concern hit home when he lectured me about the necessity of my taking care of myself and the baby I was carrying.

"Claudia," he said, "is dead!"

Sylvie, a high spirited, lovely, caring friend, spent every evening with me. I'd passed a very restless night and toward morning became awake enough to realize although only in the eighth month, I was in labor. Sylvie was running late but agreed somewhat skeptically, to make a telephone call to Corinne from the *Metro* station *before* getting on the train. Thankfully, she made the call as promised.

The Color of Dusk

She later told me that she'd almost, decided to take the train and call from her work because she felt I had been too calm to be in labor.

Corinne apparently was impressed by the calm of Sylvie's message. She showed up three full hours later. By then the contractions were about six minutes apart. I was having a great deal of difficulty sitting up in her very little *Simca Mille*. We made it to the hospital, *Baudelocque* in about forty-five minutes.

The hospital entrance was a very long hall, or so it seemed. I was forced to stop three times because of the contractions. They checked me and told Corinne it would probably be a few hours. She could come back later.

Within fifteen minutes of her departure, I was on the delivery table with the midwives. Heavy contractions were running only a minute or two apart. When the water finally broke, I heard one of the midwives say she was afraid I was going to drown the baby before he could get through the vaginal passage.

Christopher Sean was born the 20th of April 1965, weighed four pounds. He carried my maiden name. His first forty eight hours were spent in an incubator. I was put into a special room for special attention, probably because of extreme fatigue. I had lost a little weight with my eating problem and was down to 97 pounds the day after Sean was born. At 5'9", that's not much blubber.

Two days later he was out of the incubator and we were sharing a room with another new mother. His bed was located at the foot of my bed. I had only to sit up to see him. I was fascinated when a nurse came into the room and, holding Sean by the arms, "walked" him across a table. He took steps just as though he were walking by himself although they didn't actually put his weight down onto the table. The test, they said, was to check his motor functions. They checked the rotation of the hips and told me that diapers would not need special folding. I was fascinated.

Did they do this kind of check up in the States?

Sean and I had the pleasure of sharing our room with a total of five new mothers and their babies in the two months before we

Phyllis Demarecaux

left *Baudelocque*. From there we went to a rest home in *Vesinet*, a nearby Paris suburb, where we spent an additional month. The French socialized medicine had taken care of me throughout the entire pregnancy. The policy of the company I worked for paid full salary. They, in turn, received about 50% of that sum from the Social Security system.

Had I been in the United States I am certain my pregnancy would have terminated much the same as had the first one. I would never have been financially able to pay for the kind of care France gave me. The result of all this, for someone who had been told it was highly unlikely she would ever have a child, was a son. I shall be eternally grateful.

Once home, I was on my annual one month paid vacation. I checked in with the local *Creche,* making sure that I was still on their list. They pulled the registration which asked: married, single, widowed or concubine? We settled on single. The *Creche* would be taking care of my son five working days a week. The babies were clothed by the *Creche,* so I didn't have any great expense there. The charge was based upon rent and salary but would not exceed twenty (old) francs a day. In 1965 about the equivalent of two U.S. dollars. The cost of vaccinations was also included. The publishing house I worked for allowed sick leave for the mother any time the baby was sick. Fortunately Sean was a healthy baby. A little colic but a change in formula, early on solids, and things were hunky dory.

My overhead cost of living during all those months had considerably diminished. I conscientiously saved every penny possible and with this accumulation in two years I had enough to make a down payment on a one bedroom apartment. An additional part of the money came from my land-lord at the studio. She, by law, was required to reimburse the total cost of the upgrades I had made in the studio, with her approval, minus 10% for each year of habitation. I also received four thousand old francs from the new tenant. Not as much as I had paid Sylvie, but the lady needed a place desperately and I didn't want to take the chance of losing the new

The Color of Dusk

apartment to another buyer. (This purchase would not have been possible in the States where they required a guarantee from a MAN before they would make a loan such as this to a woman. Even then, it wouldn't have been a sure thing. The widowed mother of our friend, Betty Chadderdon, in Sidney had inherited a series of apartments plus a furniture business and all that was in it and yet, a local bank refused her request for a $3,000 loan to fund her daughter's desire to establish a shoe store. She was told she would have to get a man to guarantee her daughter's payments. She did. The man was jobless but being a male made him, according to the bank, more reliable than a mere woman.)

My new apartment was located on the *rue Nicolas Houel* near the *Gare d'Austerlitz* in the fifth *arrondissement*.

A nursery school on *rue Buffon* just around the corner from the apartment was another plus point. They surprised me when I came to register Sean by asking me to bring him over for an interview. He was only two years old and with the mix of French outside the house and English at home, he wasn't doing much talking. I didn't expect it to be a problem. He had been well potty trained before he could talk.

Potty time at the *Creche* was scheduled for 6 pm, the hour I usually arrived to pick up Sean. The large room with its oversized bay windows and granite tiled floor was visible from quite a distance. I could see the babies as I approached the building, each one seated directly on his little potty, no chair was involved.

They were playing tag, their little feet going a mile a minute and sometimes their hands helped speed them in all directions around that granite tiled floor. Watching them was a gleeful, happy moment for us all.

I brought him over to the kindergarden for the interview. He passed the test. I don't recall a charge so if there was one, it had to have been minimal.

It was a bathing incident that woke me up to the necessity of speaking French to my son. He was in the bathtub. I tossed a wash cloth to him and said, "Wash your face." He looked at me and with

169

Phyllis Demarecaux

a seriously quizzical expression, then cautiously raised his bottom end and began washing his *"feces."*

My son didn't know one end from the other! We both had a good laugh.

First I bought a television set. Second, I registered for the noon hour class at the *Alliance Francaise* because I was still making mistakes with the masculine/feminine genders and felt stricter attention to my use of the language would help. (For the uninitiated, everything has a gender in the French language. For example automobiles are feminine. Television is masculine. Bread is masculine and a bottle is feminine. The wine in that bottle is masculine.)

The introduction to television in our home was watching Neil Armstrong descend a ladder from the spaceship. As he took man's first step on the moon, we heard him say, "That's one small step for man...... one giant leap for mankind."

CHAPTER TWENTY-TWO

Christiane had apparently moved and left no forwarding address. Almost a year had gone by before Corinne told me that Francois and Christiane were married. It was no surprise to me, but where were they living? The residence telephone number was unlisted and Corinne couldn't remember.

She didn't want to remember. She seemed to be leery of my friendship with Christiane. Although she never expressed it, I felt she thought that, should I develop a friendship with Christiane, I would no longer be her friend, but she finally came through with their address.

Once Christiane and I got back together, our friendship blossomed. She was a beautiful woman, inside and out. Corinne, I learned had been at their wedding and had tearfully admonished Christiane for "taking Francois away" from her and that explained her reticence about giving me their address.

By now, in addition to her daughter, Maika, she and Francois had two children, a girl, Ann, and a boy, Jean.

Jean was approximately the same age as my son, Sean. The boys enjoyed each other and became fast friends. Somewhere in that time span, Christiane and the Count separated. Christiane and the children remained in the apartment, temporarily. Francois went off with a skirt, Christiane said.

She referred to this new woman in his life as "Hot Pants". There was no divorce. Francois was Catholic.

Phyllis Demarecaux

Christiane herself was destined to meet an Englishman, Leigh Chapler, who I would describe as the love of her life. Leigh was a good looking chap with deep rich blue eyes, long swooping black lashes and an abundance of risqué, but tasteful humor and charm. "Bloody" is the only word I remember ever hearing him use and that was when he was upset which was not often. He was a financially successful, international salesman and a snappy, classy, dresser. Christiane began traveling with him: South America, Central America as well as almost all the north African countries.

I had become friendly with an American author and businessman, Peter Studner, whose children's books had been published at ODEGE. I was also working with Peter on his first novel. (It was later published in the Ivory Coast in French. In my opinion, I had over edited the English edition and told Peter. He did not agree with me, so we left it as it was.) He, myself, with Christiane and Leigh, went through a brief period of socializing. Dinners and dancing in the various clubs into which Leigh always seemed to have entry.

Jean Charles Badiet had come into my life when I purchased the apartment in the fifteenth *arronidssement.* His business, Badiet *Tapis,* was just a couple of blocks away and it was his company which laid the new carpeting in my newest home. We were not lovers as some thought, but like Peter, he was just a very good friend and like Peter, he occasionally brought the lady in his life to meet me. What did I think of her?

We kept in touch mostly by telephone, an occasional lunch or dinner and on one occasion, I accompanied him on a trip to Brussels. On another he took my son, Sean, along with his nephew, to sail boats on the pond in the *Jardin des Tuileries.* Our relationship might possibly have gone beyond the good friend stage if he hadn't been twelve years younger than me. I had this thing women often do about age. Unlike men and younger women, we tend to stick to men who are older than ourselves. Personally, I feel it's because men, in a combination of almost certifiable aspects, are less mature than women.

The Color of Dusk

When Madame Turquois, the lady who owned the studio in which I was renting, put it up for sale on a reverse mortgage, I signed for the purchase of my office, which was on the court side and the small apartment on the third floor which faced the *rue des Carmes*. A slight mistake in my bookkeeping left me biting my nails. I would have to come up with 15,000 francs in cash for the initial signing which was one month away. I needed at least two months and asked Jean Charles if he would be able to help with a loan. He agreed and I was greatly relieved.

Three weeks later, with the signing scheduled for the next morning, I had neither heard from nor seen him since our conversation. I prayed. It was dinner hour when the doorbell rang. I opened the door and there he was, checkbook in hand and pen poised. "How much did you say it was?"

Three months later I got a call from him asking, breathlessly, if I had enough to cover the loan. I did and he sighed in relief. I was to go over to the store, ask for their treasurer and give her the cash. He'd taken the loan money out of company funds and they were not happy with him.

CHAPTER TWENTY-THREE

Another American friend was gone. My letter to him was returned with a stamp with which I was now familiar: DECEASED.

According to the publisher of his most recently published book, EACH OTHERS VICTIMS, written under a pseudonym, he had come down with a fatal case of hepatitis while in Rhodes, air rushed back to the States but was dead within four days.

He had suggested Sean and I spend our vacation with him during his stay in Rhodes. The timing was wrong, but the offer was generous. Would things have been different if we had been there? I don't think so.

Rue Nicolas Houel was our home until Sean was in the first grade. I sold the apartment with a comfortable increase over the purchase and along with an additional 1% interest loan offered by the company for which I still worked, I was able to go from a one bedroom to a two bedroom apartment.

Although Sean's new school was a mere block or two from the new home we decided not to transfer schools so close to the end of the year. Completing the current school year at *rue Buffon* meant taking the *Metro*.

The *Concierge* at *Nicolas Houel* would take care of him after school hours until I could pick him up.

It was about a year after our move that Sean was not feeling well. He was not a complainer and insisted he was okay to go to school anyway. It wasn't anything catching he said. "I'm not sneezing." His

The Color of Dusk

appetite dropped to nil. Two days stretched to four. I managed to get him to swallow a little broth. Although he didn't complain of any pain I decided it was time to see our family doctor. Everything seemed to be in order so blood was drawn. The nurse called that evening about seven pm with the results. Again, nothing abnormal.

His serious discomfort set in that night. Around four in the morning, his third or forth trip to the bathroom, I did a rectal. The passage was clean so I called *S.O.S. Medecin.* The SOS doctor, after talking to Sean, prepared to do a rectal. I told him there had been no stool, Sean was clean, at which point he recommended I get over to the children's hospital immediately.

X-rays showed a large pocket of puss swirling around the appendix. Emergency surgery was scheduled immediately. I was sent home to rest. The doctor would call me. I went to the office to report in, then went home. The phone was ringing when I walked in. It was the family doctor who was beside himself. His nurse had called with the wrong test results. Sean's white count was dangerously high. It calmed him down when I told him that Sean was in the hospital and the surgery was in progress if not complete. I would keep him posted.

Sean spent nine weeks in recuperation. The first two were in Intensive Care. It was a large private room with windowed walls on three sides. There were no closing stitches. Tubes drained the poison from his abdomen. He looked ghostly white and my nervous pacing put a great strain on him. He finally asked me to stand still and I realized how much my comportment was going to, at least psychologically, effect his ability to get better.

I was instructed how to clean and change the dressing over the wound and once he was able to get up and walk around, he was allowed to come home.

Things were going smoothly in our new home. Sean was back in class. Yes, life was again beautiful when suddenly there was a major upheaval at work. Our company, the mother company, ODEJ, now called ODEGE, which produced the product, would be merging

175

Phyllis Demarecaux

with its subsidiary, *Le Livre de Paris,* which sold the product. Together we would all be moving to the suburbs. There would be a lowering of our salaries, because we, in the mother company, about 30 employees, were being paid at higher salaries for equivalent jobs in the larger company of several hundred. There would be four or five months at *Carmes* before the transfer was complete but the move meant I would be forced to quit my job. No way would I have been able to get Sean to school and make it into the suburb, even by *Metro,* then return home evenings in time to care for him. The company had no flexible hours.

All this and I had so recently bought a larger, more expensive apartment. I prayed harder and longer every day.

My salary was immediately lowered but the company paid a bonus for moral prejudice, tax free as I recall, which left me feeling somewhat, if only temporarily, better. The personnel in the larger company, the *Livre de Paris,* were not happy with this solution and voted to strike.

I was, during this period, still working at the *rue des Carmes* address, but the change was rapidly approaching. Four months later the employees of *Le Livre de Paris* were back at work. They had settled the strike to their satisfaction and as it turned out, mine too. My salary was now back at the level it had been before the decrease but in six weeks I would be on the street, looking for a new job. I can't say I panicked but my stomach was in a bit of a turmoil. In situations like this praying was always the solution.

Because I was not quitting, but being forced out of my job through conditions imposed upon me by my employers, there would be a settlement.

My prayers had been heard. The settlement was astonishing.

I was paid the equivalent of one month's salary for each of my ten years of employment plus, as an above the line employee, three month's advance notice and a month's paid vacation. All this meant a total of fourteen months tax free salary!

ODEGE had also carried a small profit participation clause which netted me nine thousand francs or about eighteen hundred dollars,

The Color of Dusk

not tax free. Friend Corinne was now with the AIIC (*Association International des Interprets de Conference)* and thought it would be a good idea to start a business for organizing conferences for the many international private companies which, like the international governmental organizations often required the use of interpreters. She and another interpreter friend, Irene Testot-Ferry would be my collaborators, teaching me the ropes, the rules, etc. and my windfall would finance the enterprise.

The plan, from my point of view, was a bit financially lopsided but once again, my prayers were answered.

Corinne, just back from the general conference in Nirobi, Kenya, was having dinner with Sean and I…She was a frequent dinner guest…when suddenly I found myself saying, "I'll start a secretariat, a booking agency."

Stunned. Where did that come from? God was again on my side.

I began by contacting a good number of the various international organizations which used interpreters on a regular basis. While these organizations did have what they called permanent interpreters, they were called upon almost weekly to engage free lancers for the many multilingual conferences which took place, some annually, others quarterly.

UNESO, The Council of Europe, the World Bank, the OCDE, the European Broadcasting union and the World Health Organization were among the first organizations to which I announced my existence. Should they have problems locating the interpreters they needed, they could call on me.

From there I prevailed upon the good faith friendship of a few AIIC interpreters. Seven of them agreed to go along with me. I would maintain their work calendars and, in their absence, use *carte-blanche* to accept the offers made for their services.

Things were working out well. A little free lance work for the publishing house, a slow but steady increase in the number of interpreters I was representing was enough to pay most of the bills. In fact, two years later, all the bills. One of my interpreter clients,

Phyllis Demarecaux

Jimmy Poole, was a great advertisement for me. He told everyone that his work load had increased 10% through using my services.

A visit from brother Michael and his wife, Peggy, came as a welcome surprise. They'd sold their house in Spokane, Washington. Peggy had never been far from home, so because the family they were hoping for, hadn't yet materialized they decided to see a little of the world. I was their home base. They traveled into Italy, Spain, Greece and the Scandinavian countries. Probably England as well.

Once they settled in Paris for their final sight seeing, I sent them off on a tour of the *Chateaux de la Loire*. Sean, whose English was minimal, went along as the interpreter.

Back in Paris for a last visit before returning to the States, we dined at the Lido and enjoyed their show with Sean's father. My business was going well, so well that I no longer had the time or the necessity for doing other work on the side.

Friend Hughes de la Forcade suggested his sister might be interested in working with me. It was not my intention to hire an employee nor did I want a partner. I liked working alone. If mistakes were made I knew who to blame, but I did show Chantal the "ropes" and after spending two weeks with me in apprenticeship, she opened her own secretariat. My first full time competition. Within six months of her opening I had increased my business to what I felt was a maximum. Our father had often said, if you want to try something new, find yourself some competition. They'll do the advertising for you, but you'll get the benefit because you were there first.

My former mother-in-law was visiting family in Paris and actually having dinner with me when she learned that Jacques was dead. He was under 50 years of age.

Her return trip to New York was a sad one. Jacques had taken her to the airport in New York when she left for Paris and she was haunted by the final image she had of him. He was walking in front of her stumbling under the weight of her bags. He was so frail, she told me. So frail.

CHAPTER TWENTY-FOUR

The living room of the local Catholic church rectory in the community of the *Roque Baignard* in Normandy had served for years as an office for writer/mayor Andre Gide as well as many others. A small newly constructed building had recently became the local mayor's updated office. I don't remember how, but Christiane and I discovered that the rectory was open for lease. The previous lease had been given to a veterinarian who actually used the rectory as a storage place for his deceased parent's belongings. They wanted out and would do so for a *pas de porte*. With Leigh's help we bought our way in, 15,000 francs each. I signed an eighteen year lease and we went to work getting the place habitable.

Corrine was invited to join us but her suggestion for cleaning up the place was to hire it done. She really wasn't a do-it-yourself country girl and her interest in the *Roque* was minimal. Christiane and I, on the other hand, were engrossed in our project. Twenty minutes from the coast and Deauville, *La Roque* became our second home. Weekends were spent painting, plastering and scrubbing. Decorating was fun and the results gratifying.

A lot can happen in eighteen years.

Sean, my son, and Christiane's children, Jean, Anne and Maica, were growing up. Corrine's brother, Hughes, got married. I met Jean Ives de Vaubernier at the wedding, unaware that he was married. Corinne might have told me not only that he was married, but that his wife was present, but she chose not to.

Phyllis Demarecaux

He invited me to meet his parent's at their country home. They were charming and it was a pleasant visit. I was quite taken with him, however not proud of myself having learned that he was married. My discomfort increased. It had to end and did although I carry a soft spot in my heart for him. We've remained friends. His marriage did eventually end in divorce and he is now a happy camper with his new and lovely wife.

Jean Charles Badiet, having married and once again divorced, was back in my life. He was a good friend.

Christmas of 1980 I met my future husband, screenwriter and producer, Robert L. Joseph. He'd been spending the holidays in Klosters, Switzerland, with friends Alan and Marjorie Bernheim. I'd met the Bernheims in Paris a few months earlier through interpreter friend, Wolfe Frank. In fact they dined at my home along with Wolfe before returning to Los Angeles. Wolfe, of Neuremberg fame, was one of the interpreters used in the trial. A first time ever for simultaneous interpretation in a major trial. I believe he'd worked with French actress Simone Signore's father who had also been an interpreter.

Actually I'd met Alan Berheim in 1960 shortly after my arrival in Paris where he did a thriving business as an agent for actors. Someone had sent me there with photos for a casting call. Alan hadn't remembered and I never reminded him.

Alan called me from Klosters. His friend Irwin Shaw, beloved writer of *Rich Man, Poor Man* and others, lived in an apartment above the Messien's jewelry store with wife, Marilyn. Marilyn was interested in purchasing Broadway rights to a play she'd seen in Paris, a play written by French screen actor, Claude Rich, *Un Habit pour l'Hiver* (Winter Clothes).

Because Robert L. had produced a number of successful plays on Broadway before moving to the west coast and the film industry, Irwin felt he'd be the man whose opinion would count. Would Robert stop in Paris on his way back to Los Angeles and take a look

The Color of Dusk

at the play? Yes, he would, but Robert's French was minimal to zero, therefore, Alan called me.

Would I go to the play with his friend?

Of course I would.

Writer, producer, Robert, it turned out, was the less favored son of New York lawyer, politician, Lazarus Joseph, one time State Senator, Attorney General and eventually Comptroller of New York City. Robert had what I call a Jacky Gleason syndrome, a rich, biting humor which served to cover the deeply buried hurt of his youth. Like a lot of the writers I'd met, he drank too much. Vodka, in Bob's case. Unlike a lot of writers, he was seriously overweight.

Out of his element in Paris, his insecurity hummed through the telephone line when he called. Yes, I told him. I was Phyllis and confirmed that I would pick him up at his hotel at whatever time he stipulated.

He later reminded me that I'd been wearing a deep blue colored cape and from his point of view, I swept into the hotel lobby like reigning royalty. Not the likely person his friend Alan had contacted, he told himself and he'd dropped his attention back to the newspaper he had been perusing.

The *Concierge* pointed him out to me. I walked over and introduced myself. He looked somewhat surprised, but quickly overcame it and stood. All three hundred pounds of him!

"Thank you," he said, "for taking this time out for me."

Again I reassured him it was my pleasure and, I added, "You're taking me to a hit play which I haven't yet seen."

He smiled, shook my hand and we were on our way.

The play was deep thoughtful and presented a wonderful look into the identity crisis with which many retired men are confronted. Without the title that went with the job, they ask themselves, *Who Am I?*

Three major French stars of both theatre and film did a terrific job with *Un Habit Pour l'Hiver*. Unfortunately, Robert's take on it was that the majority of well known American actors would not be

Phyllis Demarecaux

likely to give up the money they made in films to do a play which, if successful, would net them little more than prestige. My own opinion said the play was too intellectual for the more physically oriented American audience.

For me, Robert was quickly Bob, which, I was told, would have given his British mother shivers of disapproval. For Bob, I was always Phyllis. We quickly recognized the shared cerebral nature of our mentalities. He pushed his return to the states back a week and we proceeded to make each other's acquaintance. Son Sean, now seventeen, was also attracted to Mr. Joseph. He found him amiable, intelligent, easy to be with and very funny.

Although I was working days, we had lunch together daily and dinner every evening in a different restaurant. Sean was invited to share at least two dinner evenings with us.

Our third day, friend Corinne joined us for dessert at the *Brasserie Balzar* where we were having lunch. Seriously intrigued because my enthusiasm was a first, she was curious to meet the man about whom I'd been telling her. She ordered a cup of coffee and a package of cigarettes.

Bob paid for the coffee and to her surprise handed her the bill for her cigarettes. "I don't finance unhealthy, bad habits, not even for people whom I dislike."

His departure was scheduled for the week end. I accompanied him to the new international airport, Charles de Gaulle. I don't recall the configuration of the building at that time. It was an incomplete work in progress, but from where I stood, above him, I could watch his progress as he made his way toward the boarding area. He must have pulled his passport and boarding pass out a half dozen times. I remember calling down to him that he'd have them worn out before he got to the gate if he kept it up. He looked up, surprised to hear my voice.

A couple weeks later Rowland Perkins and wife Sally were in Paris, taking me to dinner. Rowland was Bob's agent at CAA

The Color of Dusk

(Creative Artists Agency). He and his wife's approval, a positive opinion of me, would apparently confirm to Bob that it would not be a mistake to develop a more serious relationship with me.

We continued our exchange. I wrote letters. Bob used the telephone "because," he said, he didn't "write on spec." The nine hours difference in our time zones made it relatively simple. He called me at ten or eleven pm LA time and shared breakfast with me.

I think it was my first letter to him that cemented our future. I told him, and it was true, that he was the first man I had met in years (if ever) whom I felt I could look up to, down on and have trouble getting around. According to his closest friend, Shirley Bernstein, he roared with laughter when he read it. Shirley was the girl he should have married, he told me. Her mother and brothers, Bertie and Maestro Lenny liked him. Her father called him "clean and cut". But somehow their friendship never ventured beyond daily phone calls and major jostling. I was unable to find the explanation for it, but they called each other "Tree".

Romantic love had come to Bob with his marriage to actress, Susan Clark. It hadn't worked out with her either, so after the divorce, he had remained single.

I flew to New York City in November for a Thanksgiving weekend visit. Bob was interviewing Kurt Waldheim, the "unknowingly" former Nazi, then head of the United Nations. It was concerning a script Bob had been requested to write. He found Waldheim a bright, interesting man and was appalled some six months or so later when Waldheim's connection to the Nazi war camps became public knowledge.

It was on this trip that I discovered Bob never traveled anywhere without the photograph of his deceased older brother, Jacob Joseph. "Jackie", his parent's pride and joy. Tall, slender, muscular, and, as considered by his parents, very bright. Yes, Jackie, not bungling Bob would follow in his father's footsteps. Bob, the problem son, had been kicked out of at least three, if not five, prep schools. That he was accepted as a student in the University was, according to

183

Phyllis Demarecaux

Bob because his uncle Maurice Haft had donated serious money to them. Again, according to Bob, his eligibility was to be determined by his response to an exam he was given. They locked him in the university library and asked him to define plain geometry. Truth or fantasy even the best laid plans can go astray. He passed the exam.

World War II happened and Jackie, one of the younger, if not the youngest, Captain in the Marine Corps was killed in Guadalcanal. Bob still in the university was not notified. It was Maurice Haft's son, David, also a student there, who gave Bob the news. They immediately left for New York. According to David, when Bob's father opened the door of their apartment, he looked at his surviving son with what could only be defined as repressed anger and said, "What are you doing here?"

Was it any wonder that Bob meandered through life bearing the heavy burden of an unworthy survivor? He did attempt to enlist in the military and was briefly successful. It was his mother who intervened and he was let out.

He was, after Jackie's death, their only son.

It was a university drama teacher who Bob credited with having saved his life. It was he who encouraged him, who helped him develop a minimum of self-confidence. His Prep School hooky days, like those he'd shared with J.D. Salinger of *Catcher in the Rye,* were a part of his past. His future was now.

Christmas holidays. Sean was off to a ski trip with Christiane's son, friend Jean de Riocour. I joined Bob in Klosters, Switzerland. We became a foursome with actor Don Taylor and British wife, actress Hazel Court Taylor. None of us were skiers. We did long horse drawn sleigh rides into the depths of the Alps, stopping at isolated, rustic cottages where dozens of others, skiers and non skiers alike, gathered to share a hearty bowl of steaming soup and round crusted loafs of freshly baked brown bread. Then we were off on our separate ways, "home" through the pristine mountains of snow in time to nap and prepare for a sumptuous meal with the Rathaus

The Color of Dusk

family, Joan and Bernt, where I was to meet Dixie and her film director husband, Norman Jewison.

Bob was so pleased to be able to introduce me to some of his successful friends in show business, he actually beamed. It had been clear when we went backstage at the theatre in Paris, that he thought I knew nothing about the film/stage/acting industry. My experience wasn't as "high level" as his, but former husband, Jacques de Marecaux, worked in the film industry. While Bob's friends were more recognizable to the public, Jacques relationships were with the behind the scenes crowd. While I hadn't met them all, I'd certainly been surrounded by a plethora of guest celebrities while acting as a hostess at the company's annual Christmas party.

The major difference between 'them' and 'us' is that, in the motion picture business, their lives are more restricted than ours, more controlled in a sense. Because they are recognizable the public seems to think they "own" them. Their private lives are rarely as private as they would like them to be.

There are a few, of course, whose apparent goal is to remain in the spotlight. But for the most part the good ones, the strong ones, who have a sense of their own identity, are generally the best in the business. They manage their fame and its monetary benefits very well. Brother and sister, Julia and Eric Roberts (Lila Garrett's son-in-law), Jaclyn Smith, Gene Kelly, Peter Faulk (who had been in Bob's drama class), Don Taylor, Cary Grant, Alan Rich, Audrey Hepburn, Ida Lupino, Rock Hudson, Kathryn Hepburn and Jimmy Durante to name a few.

May rolled around and Bob was back in Paris. His script, *World War III*, had been picked up by the network. A good deal, if not all, of the film was scheduled to be shot on location. Director and friend, Boris Segal, was in Oregon scouting mountainous areas where several scenes would be played and doing some of the scouting by helicopter. The copter landed on top of Mount Hood if my 80 year old memory is serving me right. Blades running, Boris stepped outside to take a closer look around. The altitude, the thundering

Phyllis Demarecaux

swish of the blades, and a slight wind were the recipe for disaster. The copter, picked up by a brief gust of wind, was lifted, shifted and dropped back to the ground. Boris was struck by the whirling blades. The tragedy ended Bob's visit. He returned to LA immediately.

David Green was selected as the replacement director following Boris's death. In spite of his injection of a somewhat tasteless romance, the raves for Bob's film were top of the line. Rock Hudson was superb in one of his most surprising and astonishingly well cast roles as President of the United States. Apocalypse WOW! In fact the only adverse critic concerned Green's "romantic injection". He should have stuck with directing where he knew what he was doing … and he did a good job.

Summer school vacation rolled around with Sean off to Bilbao, Spain, where he spent the first month with his school mate, Emilio Hermandez and his family. His second month the two of us headed for the States. A week in San Francisco with Jacques' sister, my former sister-in-law, Titiana Kreinine, then on to Los Angeles and Bob.

To Bob's amazement, Sean was more attracted to television's *Chico and the Man* and *I Love Lucy* than he was to the beach. In part perhaps, because he'd just spent a month on a Spanish beach, but I think it had to do with the humor and the language. Although Sean was definitely fascinated by American slapstick humor.

Traditionally weekends at the beach were made for parties and we certainly kept up the tradition. They were largely barbecues, roasted potatoes, peppers, onions and lettuce salad with chicken, frankfurters or hamburgers and buns for the carnivorous. Betty and Steve Shagan, Lila Garrett, Mike Mindlin, Bob and Joan Markell and Tony Masucci were some of my culinary victims. I even ran into the divorced wife of Mark Miller.

Mark was a friend from New York City and the Escasoni days of sailing her up Long Island sound along with Jacques and Torban Johnki.

Bob had been hired to write a follow-up script for Sidney Sheldon's novel, *Rage of Angels*. As far as I knew he hadn't written a

186

The Color of Dusk

line so I simply assumed he was, as I, on vacation. Not exactly the case, I learned when a call came from Sidney asking if he might drop in to take a look at how Bob was doing.

Bob blanched when I gave him the message. He did not return Sidney's call and as the hours went by became more and more nervous. Sidney would quite naturally expect to see some words on paper. He shuddered every time the phone rang. It was my job to reply. Bob was not available. He was "working" on his script.

He became so nervous, so frantic that he gave me the jitters too. I was, after all, equally concerned about the blank pages and felt it was my presence that was hindering his work. It got to the point that with Bob shuddering at my side, and the insistent shrill of the telephone I grabbed it and to my utter amazement, said, "Sidney Sheldon's residence" at which point Bob almost had a heart attack and I folded over in hysterical laughter, when Lila Garrett's mellifluous voice came floating over the line, "What is going on with you two?"

In time I was to learn that Bob generally spent two to three months putting a script together in his mind before his pen touched the page. He said that once he'd envisioned the story, the pages with which he was confronted seemed less blank. When he did begin writing, he often produced as many as twenty pages a day!

CHAPTER TWENTY FIVE

Things went pretty fast once the pro-positive reports began coming in on me. Don and Hazel Taylor, Sally and Rowland Perkins, and even Irwin Shaw, all gave me a thumbs up. Irwin had loaned me a pre-publishers edition of a book he wrote. It was quite wonderful and struck me as being a very personal story. I mentioned my impressions when I returned the book. He sent it back to me with a wonderful autographed response.

Bob proposed marriage and I went for it.

The apartment on *Henri Duchene* and most of the furniture was sold. Christiane's now grown up, daughter Mika Manheim de Riocour was willing and exceedingly able to take over my business.

Sean had a year to go for his *Bacculauriat*. I moved him into the larger studio on the *rue des Carmes* in the fifth arrondissement, rented the court side studio, sold my car and flew off to Los Angeles.

By this time Bob must have been asking himself what he had done. He was so nervous he'd asked Sally Perkins to accompany him to the airport because, he later confessed, he was afraid he wouldn't recognize me.

Pets were not allowed in the terminal so Sally had been requested to return her dog to the car. As a result I was halfway to the baggage claim before they showed up. Sally was stooped over, struggling with a shoe strap. Bob was busy watching her. I stopped, unnoticed, and watched the two of them. My introduction to L.A.

The Color of Dusk

The 'car' they took me to was a glittering white limo with a uniformed chauffeur. He leapt to attention, greeted us with enthusiasm, claimed my baggage and saw that we were properly, comfortably seated.

Bob gave him Sally's address. He was, quite obviously, terrified of being alone with me.

Sally deemed my arrival an occasion for celebrating. On an empty stomach and a nine hour jet lag I cautiously sipped champagne from a crystal glass flute and for lack of something better to say, admired her freshly decorated sunroom. (I could smell the fresh paint.) Bob eventually caved in to the reality of my presence and suggested that perhaps I would appreciate a quiet nap.

Whatever.

I was foggy by now and with only a half filled glass of champagne I would happily have stretched out in the back of the limo.

It was not to be.

The faithful chauffeur, who was being paid by the hour, gleefully chalked up a serious series of dollar signs, beamed our return with enthusiasm. By now it was happy hour. Would Mr. Joseph like to stop at a "club" for a drink of happiness.

No, Mr. Joseph would not. We would go to his home in the Sierra Towers on Devlin Drive.

Ah! At last a place to put my head down.

A small, but adequate entrance sheltered a guest half bath to the left.

To the right a fairly sumptuous, though small kitchen was adequate, fine for a bachelor who certainly wasn't into cooking.

The intended dining room had become Bob's office. His desk and, to my surprise, the secretary who sat behind it, looked out across the expanse of a spacious living room. It's deck revealed the endless tree-lined Sunset Boulevard now sharing its name with the sky and beyond, the master bed-room with its common, but not so common in those days, walk-in closet.

Phyllis Demarecaux

My eyes literally swam back to his desk. She was a glowing healthy, gorgeous looking lady. She introduced herself, smiled a welcome and rushed for the…yes…Champagne. My nightcap, for sure. She shared the bottle with Bob in a fairly decent amount of time having been bright enough to realize I was either too tired or too uncaring to share their manufactured enthusiasm. Her presence had been a surprise to me. It was time to say good-bye,.

It was also about that time the bell rang and in walked Tony Masucci. Apparently Bob had invited him for dinner. I was expected to be the cook. It would be a simple meal, Bob explained. Tony was not fussy. There was steak for the gentlemen, spaghetti and salad.

Pasta I was familiar with. My favorite food. Memories of pasta were related to my grandmother. She cooked the first true meal I ever remember having eaten. Pasta! We'd lived on dehydrated vegetables boiled in water and/or milk with a slice of bread.

The kitchen range was electric. Accustomed to gas, where the heat is under instant control I was out of my element. Somehow the steak shuddered into a steaming mass of sizzles. Smoke quickly became overpowering in the confines of the small kitchen so, under the astonished eyes of the two happily chatting, now seriously muted witnessing gentlemen, I crossed through the living room, smoke streaming frying pan in hand and onto the outside deck.

The steak was apparently quite edible and I don't think they were just being nice. Tony was to become the future vice president of movies and mini series for NBC television. What kind of impression was I making on him. In any case, I don't remember eating the meal and probably didn't, I was so zonked out.

The next thing I remember is waking up to the warm, soothing sound of Cary Grant's voice. I rolled over and looked past Bob's bed to a television screen. It was indeed Cary Grant. He was proposing marriage to Debra Kerr at 3:30 a.m. L.A. time. She succumbed and they lived happily ever after. Movies can make it so simple.

The apartment in the Sierra Towers on Devlin Drive, it turned out, was a rental and the lease was coming to an end. Bob's idea was

The Color of Dusk

that we rent a house on the beach in Malibu while we search for a more permanent home. It was also a place where he felt he could do justice to the mini-series he was supposed to be writing as a follow up to his work on Sidney Sheldon's novel, *Rage of Angels*.

The story was to be Bob's using the characters from Sidney's novel. Later, Sidney was so pleased with the results, he wrote a lengthy letter to Bob, suggesting that he make a future for himself as a novelist.

Cynthia Lindsey had the perfect home for our first two years together. Our front yard was comprised of fifty yards of sandy beach at high tide and a magnificent, sprawling blue Pacific which spread out to infinity. There was a cement installed beach table/chair set up about fifty feet from the house where we could sit in the shade of a gigantic umbrella and wiggle our toes in the sand. It was an inlander's paradise.

The lower level of the house became Bob's office. I became his secretary/assistant and actually began writing a good share of the prose. Bob's specialty was developing character through dialogue. In that field, he was, in my opinion, a genius. AND, like many genius minds he was bereft of common sense but had an incredible storage of uncommon sense. That is probably one of the many things I found so attractive and loving about him. He had very little self assurance and no self esteem. He found it difficult to believe that people liked him or admired him as a person. He jealously protected his writing because it was the only thing about himself that he felt he had succeeded with and of which he was proud.

As soon as we were installed next door to our landlady in Malibu, Bob reported our engagement to a local news letter, the *Hollywood Reporter*.

He had apparently told them that I worked in the French Foreign Office.

Not exactly correct. I had most certainly booked interpreters for them many times, but I had also booked interpreters for French Presidents Giscard d'Estang, Pompidou and Mitterand. I'd booked

191

Phyllis Demarecaux

interpreters for the World Bank, the Council of Europe, the OCDE, UNESCO, the World Health Organization and the European Common Market, even inter-national Weights and Measure and world conferences on metal fatigue.

Conferences for just about anything that goes on in this world of ours.

Bob, the party man, threw an engagement party which was covered by the *Reporter,* thanks to his publicity specialist, Stan Rosenfield. Even Gerald Rafshoon, aide to President Carter, was present.

Once the *Reporter* published the little squib about our impending marriage Bob was besieged by congratulatory telephone messages which put him face to face with reality. Suddenly he was another person. Verbal abuse became daily and more and more difficult to live with. He was also doing a lot of drinking, vodka being his preferred "stabilizer".

I don't recall precisely what set me off, but whatever it was, it had to be pretty bad. I picked up my pocketbook and an extra pair of walking shoes and closed the door gently behind me. My walk away took me no farther than to our landlord, Cynthia Lindsey. She and Robert Patten had become good friends. They both listened to my version. Then Cynthia sympathized with me and kept me at her side while *her* Bob went next door to check on *my* Bob.

He returned a half hour later telling us that *my* Bob was now a "Basket Case".

Nothing new there.

They did, however, talk me into giving Bob Joseph another chance.

If it was the thought of marriage that was frightening him so much I told him, the marriage, as far as I was concerned, was off. He was once again my Teddy Bear and with a switch like that he became Bobby-Jo.

This is where I should explain our relationship. I had, quite early, been diagnosed with Sjogren's Syndrome, a chronic inflammatory

The Color of Dusk

disorder characterized by excessive dryness of the soft tissue in the body, eyes, mouth and mucous membranes (ref Merck Manual).

In my case it was the "other" membranes which were first affected. Intimate relationships were out of the question. Too painful. I don't know what Bob's problem was, he never explained and I never asked. Our initial attraction to each other was the difference in our brain waves, the way we thought, and the way we processed information.

It is also true that journalism had always been my favorite subject and being with a living breathing writer who made his living writing was a serious magnet. I was and still am a prodigious reader and so was Bob. I swear he read the New York Times from cover to cover every day. Although he appeared to be skimming it only, he would then tick off for me those articles which he thought I should absolutely read, giving me the title, the column and page number of the articles, by memory.

He wanted a family and a child was out of the question, so we bought a dog, a German Shepherd puppy, and named him Gorgeous. He was gorgeous. One of my favorite memories of Gorgeous was when he became the absent star at one of our beach parties.

John Houseman, with Joan at his side as usual, was late in arriving. I remember he stood blinking his eyes at me to the point where I thought he was having some kind of sight problem. I wasn't certain how to react but that I did react visually, was evident.

"It's my eyes", he expostulated. "My baby blue eyes. You can see them again!"

And I could!

Several pleats of eyelid had gone by the wayside. Actress Blythe Danner congratulated his decision to get a better view of the world, in spite of its decline. She was there with daughter Gwyneth Paltrow, her sweet, approximately ten year old, daughter. Director Buzz Kulick and his wife, Lorraine, were also among the elite along with Dido Renoir and, I think, Tony Masucci and Peter Katz as well.

Somehow amid all the admiring of John's blue eyes, our puppy, Gorgeous, had disappeared.

Phyllis Demarecaux

Bob was frantic. Everybody was drafted for the search, even John who said with his new eyes, he could no longer be excused. Young Gwyenth gave her search more time than any of the others. As I recall she'd been running up and down old Malibu Road, maybe even knocking on doors. Her heart was thoroughly committed.

With draftees dropping out and getting back to the social pleasures of conversation and food, Bob felt compelled to offer a bottle of Crystal Champagne as a reward.

Lorraine Kulick became the recipient.

Somehow Gorgeous had been shut up in one of the bedroom closets and was busily teething on my Tilsbury sandals, the most expensive summer-time footwear I had ever gifted myself!

CHAPTER TWENTY SIX

Bob's downstairs office was complimented with a deck which ran the full width of the house. I could sit out there and wiggle my bare toes in games of tick-tack-toe in the sand or put Gorgeous on a long leash. With it he could race after the balls I threw, retrieve them and bring them back to me wagging his tail excitedly. He'd drop the ball and wait for my next toss.

Things were settling in when the winter storms of 1982 began. One of the first things that went was the very secure cement beach umbrella, table and chairs. At least eight feet of the height of sand had been washed away by the time the storms subsided. It was as though they had never existed. I could now stand under that same deck, a full 5'9", stretch my arms upward and still not reach it. The distance of the water from the house at high tide was now no more than twenty yards at the most.

It was one of those stormy days that I invited my mother to come visit us and to meet Bob. Our conversation continued as I watched the havoc being created outside our front door. A gaily flower colored davenport was bobbing its way enthusiastically past our house. It sat upright eagerly inviting us to hop on and enjoy the ride. Each wind-whipped wave struggled for attention until, at last it flipped upside down. The game was over. The cushions, freed from their enclosure, spread apart and literally flew off in diverse directions. It was quite spectacular. I don't think Mom absorbed the gist of the information I was feeding her. It was all so unreal. In any case, and

Phyllis Demarecaux

to my surprise, she agreed to come visit us. No precise date was set because of the storms.

It was on one of the earlier days of the storms, that I had assisted a family just up the road with the evacuation of their belongings. The house, it's front foundation of useless pillars hanging in the air above the sandy beach, had been condemned. Myself and at least a half dozen other people, worked frantically to beat the incoming tide.

Mr. Gonzales, our neighbor to the immediate left had been having work done on their deck and heavy duty boulders were brought in to stabilize the house's pillar-like foundation. I was later told that he and his wife were celebrating her fortieth birthday and he was snapping pictures of her to commemorate the occasion. He'd backed against the deck rail, leaned on it, and fell onto the freshly placed boulders below.

The construction crew had positioned the rails in place but had not secured them!

The sound of the crashing waves of the incoming tide, left Bob and I unaware of the drama next door until the ambulance showed up. Our house, they announced, was the only one in close proximity which still had a stairway leading to the beach. All the others had been washed away. They requested our permission to get to Mr. Gonzales. I lead the way and somehow ended up with them. I don't recall why. We found Mr. Gonzales under his deck. He was, of course, at the least, unconscious. Increasingly stronger waves were threatening to pull him out to sea. The two medics asked that I hang onto Mr. Gonzales while they went to get a stretcher. (Why they came down there without one, is still a mystery to me.) I remember taking off my gold wristwatch and ramming it into my hip pocket to protect it from the water. Silly. The waves at their highest thrust as the tide came in, were up to my waist by the time the two returned. I'd been so busy brushing the foam from the angry waters away from Mr. Gonzales' face that I hadn't realized I'd put myself in jeopardy. I do not know how to swim. It probably wouldn't have helped if I did. The unbelievable strength of water was seriously pulling on me

The Color of Dusk

and the certainly defunct, Mr. Gonzales. I realized by now that he was dead, but it didn't seem right to let that dirty foam run over his face. The medics arrived and took over.

"Now's the moment to get out of here," one of them shouted above the roar of the waves. The formerly beautiful blue Pacific was sucking its filthy sand loaded water from beneath the deck, building an even greater wave for its next attack.

They lifted the stretcher with Mr. G. and raced toward our still standing stairwell. I rushed behind them and into the house where I found Bob praying that nothing had happened to me. Somehow I had neglected to tell him that I was going along with the medics.

A brief snack and Gorgeous was wanting to go out. It was then I discovered they hadn't taken Mr. Gonzales up to the street, but left the stretcher with his body on it, outside our back door. No place to take the dog. I went up to the street and asked them to move Mr. Gonzales so that I could take the dog out. They agreed to do so and did.

Back in the house, I called Gorgeous and out we went. Gorgeous, quicker than I, realized the gate leading to the street above was open. He bounded up with me galloping after him whereupon, reaching the top, I stumbled and fell almost face first across the body of Mr. Gonzales who was now covered with a yellow tarp which was billowing life-like, in the breeze. Eerie. A policeman on the street outside, helped me recoup Gorgeous. I thrust the dog inside the house, went back to the policeman and asked what on earth was taking so long. Poor Mrs. Gonzales must have been going out of her mind.

It was then I learned that anytime a person dies at home the homicide division has to be called.

Another stormy day I was working downstairs with Bob when I looked up and found myself facing a wave which must have been seventeen feet high. The most threatening wave to date.

"Would you look at that!" I breathed in awe.

Phyllis Demarecaux

My Bob's reaction was to rush to the window to get a better look. The wave was thundering its way toward us at the speed of a high powered cannon ball. My reaction was to crouch up against the back wall, getting as far away from the window as possible.

The wave hit!

A fountain of filthy water sprayed upward separating Bob and myself and ran across the entire length of the room. The foundation had cracked under the force of the attack.

And then it was calm.

The two of us were rendered temporarily speechless. I did a room survey. Most things looked normal.

Dirty but normal.

Probably thanks to the weaker foundation, the windows had not broken. The glass, however, was now sitting about four inches below the top of the frame that had been holding it in place.

Upstairs, the glass doors to the deck had been open. Cynthia's proud new white sofa which sat at least six feet from the door, had been sprayed with the filthy water from that gigantic wave. Earlier estimates of seventeen feet high had been a bit skimpy. To have covered the distance of the upstairs deck width, plus the distance of the sofa from the open door meant that it had to have been at least twenty feet high. The sofa was on the second floor. The lower ceiling was eight feet high and ground level in front of the house was about eight feet. You do the addition.

Somewhere in here we left the beach and moved into a house on Devlin Drive, just above Sunset Boulevard and not far from Bob's old apartment in the Sierra Towers.

We were working two scripts in those days. One about the hostages at the American embassy personnel in Iran which Bob said would never go to film. The reportedly confidential documents which had been furnished to us were too revealing and also, as I recall not particularly flattering to Mr. Kissinger. The best part of the job was that he and Robert Markell of CBS were flown to Plains, Georgia to shake former President Carter's hand. I have an

198

The Color of Dusk

autographed picture of the President with my name misspelled, probably because Bob didn't know how to spell deMarecaux when he made the request. It also seems to me that Bob managed to get his friend John Furia hired to do a section of that script. In any case, it never went to film.

The other script was the follow-up of Sidney Sheldon's *Rage of Angels*. This script became *Rage of Angels: The Story Continues* another miniseries by Robert L. Joseph.

Our life together was *very* together. Bob made it his business to get me employed wherever he was working. Since he did all his writing by hand I became his official typist.

Rage of Angels: The Story Continues was shot on location, and, yes, I was a part of the crew. I think it was Charlie Goldstein, at Fox, who said I was the biggest bargain of all. I kept Bob working a straight line. It was a lot of fun and a lot of work. I was also given a small speaking part in this follow up. It was a short scene with the Vice President, Ken Howard, and a group of dignitaries listening to a French speaker. The speaker was myself and the dialogue was my own. Because I was a member of the Actors Guild I was paid minimum for the acting, but no one ever paid me for the dialogue I wrote. Do you suppose it's too late to file a complaint?

One of Susan Sullivan's scenes was scheduled to follow mine. We met in the doorway as I was walking out. She thrust out her hand and whipped the tie of my silk blouse out. "This," she almost hissed, "is what *I* should have been wearing!"

Loan her my clothes? It had never occurred to me. The Studio took care of the "stars" clothing. I furnished my own.

During the shoot, which was done on location, we sublet our home to a family named Wagner. They did well. Six forks from an antique sterling collection with twelve place settings were missing when they left. One of a pair of brilliantly colored, gorgeous bath towels which had been a wedding gift from Norman and Peggy Lloyd was also missing and a painting which today, is probably worth much more than it was then. Our CPA who had been in

Phyllis Demarecaux

charge of the rental in our absence didn't have their state or city address so I was unable to let them know of my displeasure. Maybe they'll read this. I hope so.

Jaclyn Smith, the star in the *Rage of Angels* films, is much more than a lovely face, she's a lovely, non-pretentious woman, an excellent professional actor and a great mother. She complained about nothing and in spite of some really long days always had a ready smile, a true Texas girl with, outside the movies, a soft home built drawl. It was a pleasure to work with her. I asked her for an autographed picture, but, I specified, I want the "girl next door". It was three months after we'd wrapped up the film that her picture arrived. With everything she must have had on her mind in her busy life, she remembered. She was wearing jeans, a white blouse and sitting in an arm chair with her legs draped over one side. Just great!

Bob's next big excuse for not working was his sudden need to get acquainted with the family in which he had gotten himself entangled. When I mentioned this habit of his to Paul Miller of Universal, he told me that in the days when working as a salaried script doctor to the studio, Bob had a sign on his office door which read: I pay for interruptions.

Yes, he thrived on interruptions.

Mom came first. I did the Universal Studios tour with her but mostly she was happy to be around Bob. He loved interruptions and seemed to enjoy his conversations with her. She was no longer drinking. In fact, she had cured herself without the help of AA in 1969. She committed herself to the Montana State Asylum and for three months, worked with the young people who were battling drug addiction. Sean was four years old at the time.

Bob wasn't drinking either, at least not openly, which was okay with me. If I'd let him know that I was aware of what he was doing, he would have drank considerably more. As it was, he thought he was getting away with something, so he was careful not to overdo his intake.

The Color of Dusk

Brother Mike and his family, wife Peggy, sons Ira and Ryan and daughter Bonnie joined us a week or so later. Bob's work at the time was, I think, a script for producer Dan Blatt. *Privileged Information* had become *Sworn to Silence.* Dan I loved because he stood up to Bob's bullying. The evening we met is, for me, particularly memorable. He'd made a seven o'clock appointment to meet with us in our home. He showed up about 9:30 pm. Bob opened the door when the bell rang, but he didn't let go of it. "We've been waiting for you for two and a half hours!" he barked. Dan ducked under his arm and pushed his way into the house.

"And I," he said, "have been waiting for you for two years!"

A second of surprise then we both broke into laughter.

What Dan said was true. He'd been waiting for Bob to become available.

Dan was pretty much a regular in those days. There were several week end visits, some along with his daughters, Jessica and Chelsie. They were good company for Bonnie.

Ryan found a neighbor boy closer to his age and paired off with him.

Ira was the thinker.

They were all housed in a not luxury but adequate studio-like apartment attached to the garage which faced the street. Mom was in the main house with Bob and myself.

While our mother was now sober, she wasn't exactly socially syncopated. The day friend Jack Sacks ask "How are you?" She replied, "What do you care? You don't even know me."

And she was totally incorrect when sister-in-law Peggy was around.

One particularly beautiful morning Bob, myself and mom were having breakfast in the main house when Mike and family walked in. Peggy greeted us with "Good morning!"

"Was until you got here," my mother snarled, still jealous of her daughter-in-law, three grandchildren later.

Phyllis Demarecaux

Peggy let it slide off her back with a shrug. She was apparently more accustomed than I to our mother's seriously vicious tongue.

Somewhere in here, Sean showed up baccalaureate in hand. He'd even gotten a "mention". A mention in France means he passed a very tough exam the first try. He spent a few short weeks with us but life with Bob became too difficult. Bob was jealous of the time I spent with my son, and once again felt threatened that I would leave him. Sean was registered with the UCLA (University of California, Los Angeles) and it was necessary that I drive him to and from his classes. From our home I moved him into what turned out to be a flea bag of an apartment a few blocks down on Sunset Boulevard. Ultimately, I bought him his dream and registered him at the Berkley College of Music in Boston. His main interest had always been music. He'd taken a course in drumming with the Agostini school in Paris when he was about ten years old. I went with him to Boston, purchased the drums necessary and got him settled into the dorm, then returned to Los Angeles and a somewhat overwhelmed Bob. He found my reappearance unbelievable. He had been sincerely convinced that he would never see me again.

By the time we'd worked our way through Hemingway's *The Sun Also Rises,* I was assistant to the producer. This too was shot on location. A thoroughly professional Jane Seymour was our star followed by Hart Bochner, Robert Carrodine, Ian Charleston and Leonard Nimoy of Startrek fame. It was a happy time for me because a good deal of this miniseries was filmed in Paris. The long work hours didn't make socializing easy but I did manage to see a good many friends during the months of our stay.

One of those friends, actor/writer/interpreter, Augy Hayter, son of painter, William Hayter, auditioned during casting and ended up with a small speaking role. Francois Guetary, son of Georges Guetary, the French actor who co-stared with Gene Kelly in *An American in Paris,* also ended up with our cast and later became a good friend.

The Color of Dusk

It was when shooting scenes in the *Place Dauphine* that our second unit Director, Noel Howard, introduced me officially to the French actor/singer, Yves Montand. It was here that he recognized me as the lady who tried to take his place in the popular restaurant, Lipp, some years prior. I was flattered that he remembered. He and his very talented wife, Simone Signoret lived in the *Place Dauphine*.

The shoot in Paris finished, we were off to Segovia for the bull fights.

I wrapped myself up in the crowd and watched the filming of the run. The runners were professionals. One of them lay down as the bulls ran over him. He was unhurt, but left speechless when the cameraman asked if he would do it a second time for additional footage. He would not. The bulls, he told us, were not stupid. They wouldn't let him get by with it a second time. Segovia is a definite visit if any of you are thinking of a vacation in Spain.

The disappearance of my son overshadowed most of my time in Segovia. A letter I wrote to him was returned.

I contacted friend Michelle Lebreton in Paris because I knew she would soon to be on her way to visit friends in the States and her visit would include Boston. I asked her to contact the school to get in touch with Sean and alert him of my distress. It was with a positive attitude that I made my request but I was, as any parent would know, deeply disturbed.

Everything turned out well. Sean had left the room which he shared with three other young men. They were heavy smokers playing gown-up according to him. He didn't want to be a part of it. He was on his own and he was "okay".

Back in Los Angeles, we moved from the house on Devlin Drive into a Penthouse located in a high rise on the corner of Wilshire and Beverly Glenn, kattywampus from the home of our lovely, multi-talented, two time Emmy winner, faithful, gregarious, political friend, Lila Garrett.

Time was now filled with work on the Peggy Gugginheim story for Chuck Fries. His marriage to Ava became the event of our first

Phyllis Demarecaux

season. Guests, in the hundreds, were housed under a tent even the Ringling Brothers would have coveted. Chuck wowed us all with a well chosen, beautifully sung accappella love song dedicated to his Bride.

It was a time also when I met Bob's cousin, David Haft. We'd been working on a script for Aaron Spelling and were returning to the car in their parking lot when suddenly, there was David.

Nattily costumed in custom made trousers, impeccable white shirt and Windsor knotted tie. The complimentary jacket, folded over his forearm, bespoke of a warm summer day. His father, Maurice, had made his fortune in the clothing industry. Swansdown and Little Missy Knit Wear were two of his trademarks and son, David, was a walking advertisement. He and Bob hadn't been speaking to each other for a number of years. As I understood it, from Bob's lips to my ears, when David's father Maurice Haft died, Bob dubbed David the "Heir Apparel". David had found Bob's quirky sense of humor unpardonable.

There was no getting around it. The moment, though not quite tense, wasn't what I'd call cozy but Bob introduced me. Their greeting was brief, but civilized. And we were on our way.

The next brunch we set up, I included David and his wife, Roberta, on the guest list. Bob was surprised, but wasn't against it. His conclusion was that the fact David had verbally accepted the invitation did not necessarily mean he would show up. I, being my optimistic self, was sure he would. Any number of the guests, if they didn't know David personally, would know who he was. Sally and Rowland Perkins, Chuck and Ava Fries, writer Bob Lewin, Tony Masucci, Mort Lachman, Michael Nourri, Bob's only good friend not in show business, Jack Sacks, my friend, Susan Perkins whose father, a movie stunt man, had worked for practically everybody at the Fox Studios and, of course, Lila Garrett, would serve as a comfort cushion.

Things worked out beautifully. Not only did David show, he arrived with wife, Roberta and their son Derrick.

204

The Color of Dusk

The brunch led to a later invitation from David to join him at his winter retreat in Aspen, Colorado. Cousin Richard Haft would also be there. We went, of course. The relationship with cousins David and Richard was back in full swing. They were happily bickering on the telephone almost daily. In fact, their renewed friendship led me to contact other members of Bob's family: Judge Robert Haft and his wife Vickie, Mel and Elsie Jane Haft Estroff and Ellen and Jay Haft.

Bob had been getting treatments for diverticulosis, a colon problem, and begged off a couple of evenings while in Aspen. He wasn't exactly in pain, just not feeling comfortable.

We were back in Los Angeles when he woke me around four am, shivering and glistening with sweat. I took one look, called his doctor and an ambulance.

Three hours later he was back to being his chipper self. Three very frustrated doctors were tip toeing around the foot of his bed. Two were surgeons, plus his GP, Marty Shickman.

For the third time, Bob was asking: "What are my options?"

Speechless, the three doctors looked at each other in dismay. What more could they say?

Apparently nothing, so I did.

"Your first is cremation!" I told him.

His reply: "How soon do we operate?"

The surgery went well. The "bag" would be temporary. How temporary? Three months minimum, GP Marty Shickman told him. Now Marty knew Bob pretty well, and he realized, in retrospect, that he should have said six months, or at the least four. But he had said three and three it would be. Bob would have it no other way.

The second surgery also went well. The surgeon's team of xterns, interns or residents, whatever the case may have been, showed up the second day following the surgery. One of the young men, shorter than the others, hoisted himself up onto Bob's bed. They asked a few questions, Bob told them a few jokes, they thanked us and began to leave. The young man who was sitting, placed his hand,

205

Phyllis Demarecaux

probably inadvertently, over Bob's stomach and gave himself a push off the bed.

Bob all but howled with pain and told the young man, no holds barred, what he thought of his 'doctoring'. It was verbally brilliant because Bob never used profanity, never used God's name in vain. In fact, he was a major story teller, whom I had never heard tell an off color joke. His tirade had been dutifully reported to the surgeon who later entered the room to give Bob a piece of *his* mind. His interns were to be treated with respect.

"When they merit it, of course," was Bob's only reply.

About two weeks later I was helping Bob into a tuxedo for a special dinner when I noticed a 'break through'. A little walnut sized area was peaking out on his tummy. The stitches were coming undone. His surgeon had suggested he do sit ups! I stopped that nonsense immediately. The walnut became a melon-size and was very soon a monstrous abdominal hernia, thanks to a thoughtless intern. Friends suggested a law suit but that was not Bob's style. "We all make mistakes," was his answer. When I asked for a copy of the surgeon's notes, they were not forthcoming. The hospital remained mute, but neither we nor medicare were ever billed for the surgery.

His weight had gone down to a mere 252 pounds. The Writer's Guild Health people told me they would be sharing some of the expense should Bob want to have it taken care of surgically but he refused. Two surgeries were enough. He didn't care what he looked like, he said. He felt good. He would finish his life with that monstrous hernia protruding like a ten month pregnancy.

CHAPTER TWENTY SEVEN

By summer we were back in Malibu living in lawyer, Joan Levine's grandfathered house, a small, by Malibu standards, three bedroom rental at the beach on Old Malibu Road. The 'new' road, if there was one, must have been the one that led to the gated, much vaunted, but no different, Malibu Colony. Same beach. Same water. Bigger houses and 'bigger' names.

Weekdays were spent at the Fox studios where we were still working on *Sworn to Silence*, the script for producer Dan Blatt. It was an interesting project based on a true story, *Privileged Information*, a book written by lawyers Tom Ålibrandi & Frank H. Armania who had been assigned to represent a local killer. I actually remembered reading about the case in *Newsweek* magazine while still living in Paris and was pleased to be a partner to the script writer as well as assistant to the producer.

The bulk of the film was done in Canada. Peter Coyote, Dabney Coleman and Liam Neeson played the three major roles. Bob predicted that whoever played the role for which Coleman was selected, would be an award winner. Dabney Coleman received the golden globe award.

To my surprise Dan Blatt gave me screen credit.

When Jane's husband died she came to spend time and Christmas with us. Cousin David, Roberta, Derrick and two of David's children, Claudia and Dave Jr. from a previous marriage, were with us also on Christmas day. Claudia, David's oldest daughter came

Phyllis Demarecaux

around several times that season. Her boyfriend was an interesting character and had a terrific Goldwing motorcycle. Lila and I liked his wacky humor.

The year had brought some sadness. Jay Haft was dying. He and Bob visited regularly on the telephone. I well recall the day Jay complained about all the sympathy and get well cards he was receiving. He understood that they meant well, but they also knew he was terminal. Couldn't they think of anything else to say. How about some humor? Didn't they make any humorous cards?

Bob sent me out on a fishing trip: *Find a funny get well, or not, card.* My efforts were good in one way. I found a ten page booklet type get well card, that was quite genial. Bob had me sign it, then picked up a card with the usual 'get well soon', drew a thin line through the text and wrote in:

Hope this reaches you in time!

I think Jay was still laughing when he died.

March 10, 1990 Bob turned 67. In spite of the law against age discrimination his instinct was to get away from L.A. "before the telephone stops ringing."

It didn't take him long to confirm his decision. We would return to his early tromping, stomping grounds. We made our move toward the end of April with a touching good bye to the Commodore, our on and off, faithful housekeeper of at least six years. I'd miss the Commodore and the stories he told us about the life of his grandson, Shawn. A high school football game had put Shawn in a wheelchair, probably for life but his injury hadn't prevented him from becoming a father. He was, according to the Commodore, a young man with an outstanding lust for life in spite of the wheelchair, a God loving son of Christ.

We did a brief rental outside Great Barrington, Mass. Sister Jane, was back to spend another Christmas with us. Bob bought her a bouquet of long stemmed roses as a welcome to our temporary home. I found it very sad when she told us it was the first time anyone had

The Color of Dusk

even given her flowers. I had to admit that my first bouquet also came from Bob.

I remember that we did a pre-Christmas dinner. Cousin Billy Haft and Lila Garrett were the two guests, other than Jane, who I recall being present. There were, however, others, because I chose to do a roast beef. Unusual because Jane and I were vegetarians and Bob was well on his way, primarily because I was the cook. But the others at the table were carnivorous and I felt I owed it to them to give them a meal they would enjoy, although a vegetarian meal might have been a less memorable one!

I ate one slice of the meat and ended up with a major stomach ache. Jane ate a couple of slices with no adverse reactions at all.

New York, New York, its's a wonderful town.

Paul Roebling, our Jeremy from *Rage of Angels*, gave us the use of a one bedroom apartment in Manhattan where we hunkered down, and launched our search for an apartment. In his absence Paul had welcomed us with a center bowl filled with fruit and croissants, butter in the fridge and cream for Bob's coffee. Even the coffee pot was set up. All we had to do was push the 'on' button. I was more than impressed. The dishes in the cupboard were so expensive, I refused to eat a meal there. Breaking a single plate would probably have bankrupted me.

The ceiling in the bedroom was a masterpiece. I swear it wouldn't have been out of place in the Vatican chapel. An attractive small box (I am a box collector) immediately drew my attention. I picked it up, lifted the lid and found a collection of loose gem stones. Rubies, a plump diamond, 2 good sized pearls and a sapphire. I think I called Paul that moment and chastened him for putting me in such a tempting situation. I had known he was a great guy since the day he honked the horn at me and called me "beautiful" while we were at Fox but I didn't know he was so "well endowed."

"I didn't intend to tempt you," he told me. "My attempt was to please you."

Phyllis Demarecaux

We took an apartment in the Carnegie Mews at 56th Street and Broadway, overlooking Central Park. Parks are beautiful to look at, but they are a still life. A very still, still life.

We soon switched to a corner apartment, in the same building, one floor below which straddled Broadway and 56th Street and our view came back to life.

Up to now, we'd always rented because Bob was against the idea of being a home owner. His friend, Louis Calhern's mantra had been "buy a home and you die". My contribution to Bob's meager common sense, "Whatever you choose to do, you will eventually end up dead", was enough to reroute his brain waves. We selected a home in East Chatham in upstate New York. A home with ten acres and a pond. The pond was not visible from inside the house but that was soon remedied. I hired a builder, still in the region, to knock out a good part of the living room wall and insert a wide angled window which framed the pond beautifully. If he had any lingering doubts, Bob was seriously appeased.

He didn't swim and, of course, neither did I, but he loved to fish, he said. The pond was stocked with bass and within days I was on the casting end of a fishing pole. Bob, seated in a chair on the deck beside me, was the worm master. He wiggled them onto the hook and I did the fishing. His method was to spur me on, prompt me, encourage me, when he felt it was needed and his praise was glittering when I snared my first fryer. I had purchased a perfect knife *for him* with a blade intended only for the gutting of fish. Good thing I had, because it made the job much easier......*for me.*

I bought a riding mower and did the mowing myself. About two manicured acres. The remainder of the property was wooded. We worked on *The Choice* - which was to become *Midnight Jury* - with Judd Kinberg, producer. It was a World War II story. In my opinion one of Bob's better scripts. There were a couple of option purchases but the script never went to film. World War II stories were *passé.*

Christmas was drawing near. His working buddy, Judd Kinberg and wife Monica were taking off. Should we take off too? Montana

The Color of Dusk

was not appealing to my New York born husband. Certainly not in the winter. Why would we want to go where there was more winter? Chatham had a overabundance of snow.

I suggested we go to Paris. The idea wasn't repugnant to him. It was even attractive, but what would we do?

We'd give a New Year's party.

Who would come he wanted to know.

Well, Darlin', I lived there twenty four years and had actually made a few friends. Some of them would remember me.

And they did! My interpreters were wonderful. At least thirty of them showed up. Christiane was wonderful and so was Bob's cousin, Richard Haft, his Conde Nast friend, Daniel Salem, actors Francois Guitary and his wife Helen Fitzgerald, as well as Francois' father, Georges Guitary, still the the Gene Kelly of France, who was doing a new show in Paris for the first time in ten years. Corinne was married now and living in the south of France. There were also members of the French crew from the *Sun Also Rises,* with Jean Pierre and Christine Avice.

Daniel didn't stay long. We were on the 23rd floor in a high rise rental overlooking the Seine in the fifteenth arrondissement and as it turned out, much too high up for Daniel. The very idea gave him vertigo. Paul Roebling didn't show up but he sent a beautiful note of thanks for having been invited.

Paul was special, somewhat in the same way that Bob was special. He was definitely a man who could use a hug. While laughter brightened his countenance there was an aura of sadness that clung to him. He was happy for his son, Chris, and happy for his son's love of music but in the end it was about his wife. She had died and something irreplaceable in him had died with her.

In a scene from *Rage* Paul, as Jeremy, described the emptiness of life when love was absent. A ladies slipper sat in the center of the bedroom floor, abandoned, as was he when death had lured her away. Her presence surrounded him, a still life of what had been but no longer was.

211

Phyllis Demarecaux

Paris became a winning winter wonderful place to be. The New Years Eve party turned into a four year encore.

Paul never made it, not even to one or our New Year Eve parties, but he made up for it by flying over in the Concorde spending an evening with us and taking us to a sumptuous late dinner in Bob's favorite haunt, *La Coupole*. Bob, of course, kidded him about it. In a not so strange way, Paul was self conscious about his inherited wealth. He did shrug off Bob's tease with a quiet smile. "I thought it was time to do something for myself."

Back from Paris, we Amtracked our way to Chatham only to receive a call from Maika. The AIIC (*Association International des Interprets de Conference)* was having its fiftieth year anniversary and I was invited. This was on a Wednesday. I packed an overnighter, went back to the city and picked up my ticket for Friday. The dinner in Paris took place Saturday night and was held in one of the sumptuous buildings on *Avenue Kleber,* just off the *Place de l'Etoile.* A veritable avenue of giant glistening candelabras furnished light for the full length of an enormous dining hall. We were all dressed for the occasion. Women in long flowing gowns and men in tuxedos.

Not only did I see interpreters who I hadn't seen for several years, I met three who had worked with me, through me, but always by telephone. We were seeing each other for the first time. Maika had invited me to an unforgettable occasion.

CHAPTER TWENTY EIGHT

We were in our last winter in Paris. Bob's health was beginning to go downhill. Traveling was not easy as it had been. Back surgery left him dependent on a wheel chair for even short distances. He wasn't the kind of guy who would make any strategic effort toward helping himself. I was the helper, the wheel chair pusher. When we arrived at our destination, Bob stood and walked. He did know how to make an entrance.

We stayed a little longer than usual because Christiane wanted to make a fuss for Bob's birthday in March. We went to the rectory in the *Roque Baignard* where we spent the weekend along with Jonothan, Christiane's grandson, Maika's son. Jonothan returned to Paris. Christiane, Bob and myself treated ourselves to a visit and dinner in Honfleur before heading back. Christiane had a heavy week before her. They were doing the season's showing of the new line in Cashmeres. She was looking forward to the final closure celebration that Saturday.

Bob and I returned to New York and went on to Chatham Friday. I think it was Monday that we received a call from Maika. Christiane had been hospitalized late Saturday night. When the doctor examined her Monday morning he was unable to find a problem, pronounced her well and said she could go home. Other than feeling exhausted, Christiane said she felt well. She called Maika and asked her to bring some cosmetics so that she could make herself look human again. By the time Maika arrived at the hospital,

213

Phyllis Demarecaux

her mother was dead. Her esophageal passage had ruptured and she bled to death internally.

Christiane had suffered from esophageal acid reflux for some time. I am unaware of the medications she had been given for the condition, but I know, from my personal experience, the pills did not help me, they only masked the problem. It was an eye, nose and throat doctor who asked me what kind of diet they had put me on for my esophageal reflux. Diet? Nobody had mentioned a diet. They just put me on pharmaceuticals. For five years, from about 50mg a day to 600 mg a day! I am now on an acidic free, caffeine free diet and have no problem at all.

I flew to Paris for the funeral. It was all so unreal. The photo I had taken of Christiane and Bob as they walked away from me toward a restaurant in Honfleur, just ten days earlier, is my last image of the two of them together.

Maika and I went to the mortuary to get closure, but when I stepped into the room and saw my dear beautiful, loving friend looking, cold and old, as she never was, I grabbed Maika and pulled her away. I didn't want her to see her mother like that.

As Bob's health wasn't getting any better we gave up the winters in Paris and began commuting between East Chatham and the City. A second back surgery left him for the most part, dependent on his wheel chair. It wasn't that he couldn't walk, but his coordination made using a cane very awkward, even dangerous and he refused to be seen with a walker. His morale wasn't at its peak. His friend, Shirley Bernstein, was dying. Her faithful secretary/caretaker of years, Hope Taylor, had called to let us know that the end was near. It was a struggle to get Bob to call her. He didn't know how to confront the truth. I insisted he would never forgive himself if he didn't tell her good-bye. And so he did.

Shirley's weak voice came over the phone. "Tree?"

"Yes, it's tree here, too," he replied. "And another fine mess you've gotten us into...."

The Color of Dusk

Shirley's laughter rippled over the line. "Ah, yes," she said. "It's a good-bye for good." She rang off and, according to Hope, died within fifteen minutes.

Bob was still having trouble with the cane. He kept tripping himself. The first two times it was outside on the grass. I wasn't able to lift him on my own and with nothing around to help him push himself up, I had to resort to calling for help at 911.

The third time he fell was in the garage.

I had been in the office working on my effort to write a first book (copyrighted but unpublished, *The Maid's Room*) about my first two years in Paris. It was approaching our usual dinner hour when I glanced at the clock. Bob was later than usual. It was his thing to go to a local snack and gas shop where he ate fig newtons and drank milk while perusing the New York Times. It was when I went into the kitchen and picked up the cell phone to call him that I heard a groan.

He was lying on the concrete floor of the garage. He must have been unconscious. Although he seemed to be coming out of it, but he was not fully aware. He didn't sound quite like himself. He wanted me to help him get up. I wasn't sure if I should move him. He insisted. "Alright. If you can get to the steps, you may be able to push yourself up from there."

It sounded like a plan and he was suddenly, or seemed, more alert.

I helped him sit up. He began scooting himself along the floor. When he reached the stairs and looked up at me, blood was rushing in behind his right eye, swelling it all out of proportion. I watched, not believing what I was seeing. My voice came out a whisper. "You really did it this time, Bobby."

The responders to my 911 call were there within minutes, the benefits of a small town. Bob, still conscious, was telling them that he had to get to the bathroom. He wanted to "pee". They calmed him, said they would use a catheter.

215

Phyllis Demarecaux

The three of them agreed they needed to get him to the trauma center in Albany. I went into the house to get my coat. It was by now, near seven pm. When I came back, the ambulance had left without me. I went for my set of car keys and discovered the gas tank registering one gallon. By the time I filled the tank and left for Albany the ambulance was long gone.

I had only been in Albany once and it had been in daylight. I got onto the turnpike and once in the neighborhood of Albany, put in a phone call to the trauma center asking for directions. A young man told me I was actually about ten minutes from there. I thanked him and was on my way. Fifteen or twenty minutes later I realized something was wrong. I drove back to where I had been and called again. He was very apologetic. He realized that he'd told me to turn in the wrong direction the second he hung up, but he didn't have my number. The telephone those days weren't as informative as they are, or can be these days.

I arrived at the center and parked in a handicapped zone next to the door. Inside they stopped me at the desk. The information Bob had given to them was his address at 57th and Madison during the days of his bachelorhood and prior to his move to California. I could hear him calling for me. He couldn't have been more than twenty or thirty feet away. I started to go to him. The young lady at the desk grabbed my arm and pulled me back. "We need to get this information corrected."

By the time I got to Bob, he had gone into a coma.

Their money was more important than my need to have a last word with my husband. I can only hope he hadn't heard me when I said those fateful, haunting, last words: "You really did it this time, Bobby."

Local friends from Chatham all asked me why I hadn't called for help. I can only assume it was because I had spent the major part of my life alone. There had never been family close enough to call upon. I'd long ago learned that life's decisions, large or small, are dependent upon prayer and my heavenly director. Because of the lack

216

The Color of Dusk

of family direction in the teen years, I had become a 'do it yourself person', nobody was going to do it for me.

Bob had always been certain he would go before me. In fact I think he prayed it would happen that way. He did not want to be left alone, he said, because he knew he'd never make it without me. He'd asked that I not go to extreme measures to keep him alive. I certainly didn't want to save his life if he was severely brain damaged because whatever we may think, we do not know how much the patients understand and it would have been too painful should he live under those conditions. For himself as well as for me.

The trauma team wanted to operate. I called Doctor and friend, Michael Jacobson in New York City and asked his advice. It didn't sound to him as though surgery would be of any help other than for the doctors' research. The operation, as expected, was not a success.

Somewhere in here, I called my son, Sean. He in turn called his girl friend and now wife, Brooke Sawyer. They rented a car and she drove to Albany. Sean had been without a driver's license since living in Los Angeles. With public transportation readily available and not owning a car, he'd reasoned that he didn't need one.

The hospital had given me a room designated especially for people like myself, people who were waiting for news of injured family members. I was even able to sleep an hour or two and this is where the kids found me. Judd Kinberg also showed up. I don't know how he learned about the accident. I probably called him. Bob was transferred from the trauma center to the hospital following the operation. There were so many cords, tubes and whatever, extending from his head that he didn't look human any more.

I don't remember much about what was going on. Somewhere in that time, I asked that the life supports be pulled. They honored my request, Bob's request. They also contacted a Rabbi. She came immediately. Bob would have loved her. She was wearing a beautifully embroidered Yarmulke.

I was told to go home and wait. The hospital would call me if there was a change. Brooke lead the way home. I followed in my car.

217

Phyllis Demarecaux

She and Sean had to get back to the city for their work, of course, so I was alone. As I pulled into the garage I noticed the cane. It had been under the car. The new step up to the door leading to the laundry room had a large curved gauge in the wood. It spoke to me:

Bob had lost his balance as the door swung outward toward him. Perhaps he had tripped on his cane. It was apparent, because of the gauge in the wood, that he had attempted to save himself from the fall by hanging onto the door, but his weight was more than he could handle and he'd lost his grip. It also explained to me, the position of his body on the floor of the garage. He'd been lying on his back more past the back of the car than beside it.

Just minutes before midnight the 29th day of April, I was alone, already in bed, when the call came in. Bob was gone.

I cried.

A gentleman from the Crematory came to get information and payment. He wrote with a felt tipped pen and I asked him if he was able to read his own writing when he finished. He assured me "yes" but he was wrong. The information he supplied gave the wrong year of birth which meant that the newspapers were all saying that he was ten years older. The error was also printed on his death certificate. I had it corrected.

Then came a couple of tough looking policemen, arms akimbo, holstered pistols and clubs hanging from their waists. They were evidently prepared for the worst. They asked dozens of questions. I was still in a foggy state of numb disbelief. They exchanged knowing glances. It was intimidating. What were they doing here?

As they were leaving I said something about what Bob had said to me, or perhaps that he had said to the ambulance people. I don't really remember what it was. Their reaction was startling.

They turned in unison. *"He was alive?!"*

Of course he was alive. "He died in Albany at the trauma center." They left, their egos deflated. In retrospect I think they thought I was some kind of murderer and once I was more alert I realized that was exactly what it was all about. They were with the homicide

The Color of Dusk

division. I should have remembered what had happened with Mr. Gonzales in Malibu. These young men evidently hadn't bothered to do their research. I know that many people in the area thought I was much younger than Bob. One gentleman even asked him if I was his daughter! In reality I was only eight years younger. They also assumed that because Bob had been in show business, he had a lot of money. He didn't. We'd spent the bulk of his savings having a good retirement life. He had worried about it toward the end, but it was his money, he had earned it and besides, I told him, I was having as much fun as he was.

I called our family rescue team master, sister Jane. She came immediately. I had to get moved out of the apartment in New York City before the end of May. She would help me, physically, morally, emotionally, lovingly. She had been a widow for twelve years so she knew well what I was going through. The lease was cancelled with no extra charges. Everything was trucked to East Chatham.

The New York City memorial dinner was the first. With the exception of his cousin David, all of Bob's family lived on the East Coast, between the City and South Florida. Two of Bob's (and my) favorite doctors came to the memorial, Michael Jacobson and Gerald Smallberg. Dr. Jerry was also a playwright. A good one, in Bob's estimation and in mine.

Following the family memorial we left for Los Angeles where there was a second memorial, this time with faithful friends in show business. We used a stage at the Writers Guild where friends shared their stories of life around Bob Joseph. The speakers I remember best were writer Robert Lewin, writer/producer Lila Garrett, writer Michael Halperin, actor Norman Lloyd and actress/director Nancy Malone. We followed it with a dinner in a nearby restaurant. There were forty or fifty people there. I regret not having kept a signature book. I didn't realize how little one remembers. All this activity was keeping me from facing reality. It has also, if not a bit belatedly, made me understand the old maxim: Make no rash or major life decisions for at least a year or even two after losing a life partner.

219

Phyllis Demarecaux

Jane returned to Chatham with me. I checked in with my faithful caretaker, Willard Doyle. Willard had made our commuting life back and forth to the City possible. He took care of the house, kept our cats, Dr. Fido and Jaws, fed and happy. With everything left in his capable hands, we went off to Paris where I would introduce Jane to the city which had been my home for twenty four years. I rented a small studio on the Left Bank. We walked everywhere. It was the best way to introduce her to the ambiance, the park pleasures, the architecture and the people. Maika gave us a big dinner party. I managed to locate my American in Paris friend, Michael Morris but was unable to reach Francis Morel, a friend from my days in the publishing house. I showed her where Bob and I had given our New Years parties. His death still wasn't real to me. I hadn't left myself time to grieve.

Back home again, Jane was off briefly to Billings to file her taxes for which she had been given an extension in time without penalty due to Bob's death. Sister-in-law, Peggy said our brother needed a vacation, could she send him to us. Of course. He was with us a month. I recall renting a seriously worn out U-Haul truck, but it served its purpose. We picked up the furniture I had stored from the City and began preparing for an "estate sale".

After Mike, baby sister, Sharon, now in her 70's came and spent a couple of weeks with us. Following her visit, Don Baxter, my high school dance partner, called. He was a widower and lonesome. Jane and I decided to invite him to come see us. He accepted with pleasure. It was October if my octogenarian memory serves me right. His health was definitely not good although he did no complaining.

We picked him up at the airport in Albany. Putting Bob's wheel chair in the trunk of the car had been a lucky afterthought. We did the New York City tour and *Dieu* knows what else to keep him entertained. Don's wife had worked a great deal with pottery and apparently a good portion of his garage was stacked with her wares. He was lost without her and didn't know what to do with it. We

The Color of Dusk

agreed to stop in Fairview (Montana) on our way westward and lend him our helping hands. But first, I had to sell the house.

The decision to sell had come when I learned that Madame Turquois, the woman whose studio apartments in Paris I had purchased on a reverse mortgage, died. The two studios, one larger than the other, were located on the *rue des Ecoles* in Paris's fifth arrondissement. An ideal location, in my opinion. I regret having sold both of them. The smaller one on the court side would have been a perfect *pied-à-terre* for visits to Paris. Maintenance costs and it would have made revisiting Paris an easy, even spur of the moment, possibility.

With money in hand from the sale it was time to get the Chatham house ready for sale. The dollar value, for me, was minor. We had a mortgage which we could have and should have paid off.

Colors for this enterprise were selected from a Tanglewood brochure, green and blue. The risers on the steps leading to the front door were green. The trim around the garage doors was green and white. The garage doors themselves were the same chocolate brown as the house.

The new front door was almost the color of cedar. Inside the foyer was a deep, brilliant blue with white crown molding. The kitchen, dining area, living room and bedrooms remained an off-white, The slanted wall with the outside banister of the stairway became a deep red burgundy. The banister itself was actually a six inch wide piece of wood which matched the color of the front door with a white strip separating it from the red burgundy wall. The upstairs bathroom became a rich green with white crown molding. Downstairs the bathtub was replaced by a walk-in shower.

Our goal was achieved. We'd wanted the interior to be unexpected and it was. It did not look like the interior of a house surrounded by trees and a fish filled pond. It looked downtown, urbanized.

Everything took longer because we were doing a good deal of it ourselves. Don was getting anxious. He kept calling, wanting us

Phyllis Demarecaux

to come earlier. His health was deteriorating. By February he was back in the hospital. He had been doing some internal bleeding, he told us. His last correspondence was a lovely, somewhat romantic, valentine card.

He died before we were able to come and in the middle of reinventing the house, getting rid of furniture and needing to sell it before leaving, we did not make it to the funeral. Don had dated all three of us sisters, Jane, Sharon and myself, during our high school years. He was a good friend. We think of him often. He was a part or our growing up. His son Tom is running the business he and his now deceased brother inherited when their father passed away.

The house sold. We decided to ship the car and take the train. Sharon and husband Charles picked us up in Malta, MT. We spent three days with them, then on to Spokane, WA., this time by car. Sharon and Charles were driving. Brother Michael and his wife were hosting our stay during our house shopping experiences.

The Cadillac arrived within a week and within another week, it gave up the ghost at 80,000 miles. The first new motor was put in at the 30,000 mile checkup. It should have been declared a lemon at that point.

Repairs, according to Comp USA, would run well into the thousands. What they were saying in fact was that it was beyond repair and requested that I have the car removed from their lot at my expense. A little research within the family circle and I had myself a master mechanic who might want to give it a try. One look at its beautiful exterior and he was hooked. I said he could have the car and gave him the key, my only stipulation being that he drive over to see me once the job was complete. It took him about three months at which time I gave him my gold key. The key had been used once - the night the ambulance took Bob to the Albany trauma center. The night they left me behind.

We fell in love with a LARGE house in Spokane. It would be a dream home after having lived so many years in The Coach.

The Color of Dusk

It's perfect for a couple of loners. We use every inch of space. Jane's oversized bedroom and her office are in the walk-out basement. My bedroom is upstairs with the two guest bedrooms. Instead of using a room for my office, I installed myself at the far end of the downstairs endless family room, nothing claustrophobic about it: within commuting distance from Jane's office, but entirely set apart. I can't see what she is doing and she can't see what I am doing and that's the way we like it. We get together upstairs where we prepare, eat our meals and watch television, 3ABN, Amazing Discoveries, Proclaim, and others, listen to music and exchange ideas. The formal dining room is used only when we are more than four people.

We became potential buyers at auctions held by several storage unit facilities: people who seemed to have abandoned their belongings and for whatever reasons had ceased to pay their storage bills. It was fun while it lasted. Once we purchased a unit, we selected items for a garage sale which would cover the expense. The remainder was used to help people in need: a couple whose home had burned, a divorced mother with children and an abusive ex-husband, legal immigrants who were just beginning their new lives in this country.

We were forced to give up the practice because, I guess I could say, of our ages. Once a unit was purchased, we had 24 hours to clean it up. This worked when we had someone to help us with the lifting, but became impossible when we couldn't find help.

The last unit we purchased had a refrigerator, a freezer, television console, a dining room set, a full length sofa and book cases. It was just beyond our strength. As luck would have it, a gentleman who had just missed the bid by $5.00, asked if he might purchase the bulk of the larger items from me. A well rounded "Yes" from Jane and I and he was there the next morning with a truck, a trailer and an assistant. Because the larger pieces he purchased were stored in the back of the unit it was necessary to remove everything in the front, therefore he ended up loading our truck as well as his own.

Phyllis Demarecaux

A year later sister Sharon and her husband moved back to Spokane so now all the siblings are in easy visiting distance. It's a pleasure after having spent 55 years of my life away from them all.

I sold the truck and bought a Toyota Prius. The gas mileage decreased by five miles to the gallon when they began adding 10% ethanol to our gasoline. Nevertheless the car still gives me 51 miles to the gallon. For those people who don't yet understand, a hybrid car has a small gas engine which keeps the batteries charged in much the same way the battery on a regular car works.

Some people still ask me how often I have to plug the car in. It is a hybrid, not a totally electric car. It does not have to be plugged in. Only a purely electric automobile has to charge its batteries by being "plugged in".

We've done Christmas in Malibu with Sean and Brooke as guests either in Tom and Holly Sawyer (Brooke's parents) beach home or with Lila Garrett on Wilshire Blvd in Los Angeles, with Roberta Haft, Bob's cousin David's wife in Beverly Hills and on one occasion with my friend, Annie Studner.

I've been to France a couple times without Jane. The first time to visit my friend Claude Benoliel following his heart surgery. Unfortunately, although there were complications, his death was unexpected. Unexpected to me and to his wife, Michelle, although in retrospect, Michelle said she felt that Claude had been preparing her for the worst.

Maika has always been good about giving me a place to lie my head at night. She throws in meals as well. I love that girl. She's turned into a beautiful woman and friend, inside and out. Jane and I spent time teaching English to two lovely Ukrainian ladies. One of them, the mother of Pastor Volodie Nesternik, died of cancer. Jane still teaches Vera. I've had to stop because the Sjogrens has done a job on my vocal cords and continual talking becomes stressful and very tiring. It's my inability to sing which bothers me the most.

The Color of Dusk

We make it a point to see that the church pews are cleaned and properly stocked with tithe envelopes. We also volunteer at the church- owned Better Living Center food bank.

While Jane is giving Vera her English lesson, I am working on this book. Why did I write an autobiography? Because so many people have told me that I should.

For the moment life goes on. I love it. I love people. We're all so diversified and as long as God wants to keep me here, I'll make it my business to keep on giving (and accepting) hugs of gratitude.

There may be new adventures to come. Jane and I are both in good health but at 84 years of age, I feel I'm reaching the dusk period of my life, hence *The Color of Dusk*.

I've updated my will and prepaid my cremation. I wake up wondering what day it is. Do I do the church today? No, today is Food Bank day. *Or is it*, I sometimes ask myself. Do I have a dental appointment? Can I still touch my toes? Balance myself on one leg?

Who's coming to dinner?

Did I remember to comb my hair?

Does it matter.......?

CPSIA information can be obtained
at www.ICGtesting.com
Printed in the USA
FFOW04n0430170217
32534FF